I0814290

The Monocle Book of ITALY

First published in the United Kingdom in 2021 by
MONOCLE and Thames & Hudson Ltd,
181A High Holborn, London, WC1V 7QX
thamesandhudson.com

First published in the United States of America in 2021 by
MONOCLE and Thames & Hudson Inc,
500 Fifth Avenue, New York, New York, 10110
thamesandhudsonusa.com

MONOCLE is a trading name of Winkontent Limited

Reprinted in 2022

British Library Cataloguing-in-Publication Data
A catalogue record for this book is available from
The British Library

Library of Congress Control Number: 2020951884

For more information, please visit *monocle.com*

This book was printed on paper certified
according to the standards of the FSC®

Edited by *Chiara Rimella & Joe Pickard*
Foreword by *Tyler Brûlé*

Designed by *Monocle*
Proofreading by *Monocle*
Typeset in *Plantin & Helvetica*

Printed by *Graphicom*

Printed and bound in Italy

ISBN 978-0-500-97113-0

Tyler Brûlé: *A loving relationship with Italy*

Do you ever ask yourself, "If you could only eat one cuisine for the rest of your life, what would it be?" Or perhaps you're more partial to the holiday version that forces you to ponder, "If you could pick just one country for vacations for the rest of your days, which would it be?" And, of course, there are many more niche versions of this game that ask you to consider where in the world you'd go if you had to choose an architect or wine-maker, a photographer or fashion buyer, a carpenter or publisher.

It will come as no surprise that at MONOCLE we play this game a lot and, given the title and depth of the volume you're currently clutching, it will also come as no great revelation that Italy is the country that consistently comes out on top when you ask people to think about all the qualities, products and experiences that are essential for a perfect weekend, an easy lunch on the terrace, a perfect wardrobe, a well-appointed apartment, a smart ride through town or a speedy dash across the Med.

Our relationship with Italy is long, deep, passionate, occasionally complicated, often hilarious and always rewarding. For well over a decade, hardly an issue has passed without us photographing the works of a recently graduated furniture designer, interviewing a plucky entrepreneur from Trieste, reporting on a newly opened hotel in South Tyrol or conducting grand reportage from a less-explored corner of the country. Along the way we've worked with small manufacturers and ancient producers to develop glassware and garments for MONOCLE's shops, including our own little outlet in a cosy corner of Merano. Up and down the country we have correspondents who keep us abreast of all that's newsy and noteworthy, not to mention loyal readers who operate as an informal network of contributors on topics ranging from *bagni* to bookshops, *gelaterie* to modernist furniture dealers.

It's in this same spirit that we set out to commission and compile a book that celebrates all the aspects that make Italy a constant draw for excellence across myriad sectors of business, culture, design, media and urbanism. And worry not, there's also plenty to keep you daydreaming about lazy afternoons on a lawn on the shores of Lake Garda, lingering late into the evening in a hidden kitchen in Bologna, rambling along gravel roads in the Tuscan countryside, commissioning a little hut in a valley high above Aosta, discovering a forgotten gallery in Turin, diving off the rocks along the coast from Genoa and ending the day surrounded by chic, bronzed locals. *Perfezione!*

Illustrated Italy:
Tip to toe

From craggy mountain tops to cactus-strewn coastlines, join us for a tour of the proverbial boot.

1.
Skiers flock to Italy's 6,000km of Alpine ski runs each year, making the mountain economy worth 11 per cent of the country's GDP.

2.
From the ubiquitous Panda to flashy Alfa Romeo models, Turin's Fiat Chrysler Automobiles group produces some of Italy's most popular cars.

3.
Milan's magnificent Duomo was constructed by stone-cutters from all over Europe, using characterful Candoglia marble.

4.
The Brianza region is known for its long history of furniture production. Many brands – including Cassina, Minotti and Flexform – are based here.

5.
The Alpine ibex – or *stambecco* – can be found in the rocky terrain along the snow line of the Alps. It was once believed to have magical powers.

6.
At the foot of the Dolomites, the area of Belluno in Veneto is home to around 80 per cent of Italy's €4bn eyewear industry.

7.
Olive trees were introduced to Liguria by Benedictine monks in the early Middle Ages. Today the region produces some of Italy's best olive oil.

8.
The Italian riviera runs along the coast of Liguria from the French border to Capo Corvo. The shore is an endless succession of *bagni* (beach clubs).

9.
Prosciutto di Parma is a thinly sliced ham produced from the hind legs of heritage breed pigs, which are salted and left for months to cure.

10.
Traditionally worn during carnival, the Venetian mask was the ultimate equaliser, allowing different members of society to fraternise in disguise.

11.
Italy has some of the world's leading shipbuilders that deliver huge cruise ships for companies that sail them around the Med and beyond.

12.

The Palio di Siena is a thrilling horse race steeped in tradition, which takes place in the city's Piazza del Campo on 2 July and 16 August every year.

13.

Michelangelo's David was originally destined to stand atop Florence's cathedral but ended up at street level due to his handsome features.

14.

The Marche region has been the heart of Italy's shoemaking industry for more than a century. Big names such as Tod's and Santoni were born here.

15.

The ancient Romans were a bloodthirsty bunch: their 50,000-seat colosseum was built to hold gladiator contests and battle re-enactments.

16.

Umbria is celebrated for producing some of the country's finest red meat and salame – best washed down with a large glass of regional red.

17.

A Neapolitan invention from the late 1880s, the pizza margherita replicates the colours of the Italian flag with basil, mozzarella and tomato sauce.

18.

With only 50 to 60 left in the Abruzzo region, the Marsican brown bear is on the brink of extinction but its numbers are slowly rising.

19.

Pompeii was perfectly preserved when Mount Vesuvius erupted in 79AD covering the town in ash. It wasn't discovered for another 1,500 years.

20.

Puglia's *trulli* huts were designed to be sneakily dismantled at short notice, enabling feudal lords to avoid paying taxes on them.

21.

Adorning balconies and terraces across Puglia, these ceramic flower buds known as *Pumi di Grottaglie* are believed to bring good luck.

22.

Chilli peppers are ubiquitous in Calabria and the region's cuisine is arguably Italy's most fiery. Soppressata salame hails from here.

23.

The landscapes of southern Italy and Sicily are dotted with prickly pear cacti, known here as *fico d'India* – Indian fig.

24.

Sicilians have been fishing bluefin tuna – the world's most expensive fish – for centuries. Today 80 per cent of the catch is exported to Japan.

25.

The *carretto Siciliano* is an ornate, two-wheeled horse or donkey-drawn cart often painted with scenes from Sicilian folklore and history.

26.

The Arabs introduced oranges to Sicily around 850AD. Today Italy is the second largest producer of citrus fruits in Europe, after Spain.

27.

Europe's most active volcano, Mount Etna erupts once a year on average. Regardless, its slopes are home to a quarter of Sicily's plucky inhabitants.

28.

Sardinia's 7,000 *nuraghe* – cone-shaped basalt structures which sometimes served as fortresses – date from 1500BC to 400BC.

29.

The flag of Sardinia features the heads of four Moorish invaders who, as legend has it, were defeated in battle in 1096.

30.

Sardinian wild boar are smaller but more savage than their European counterparts and can be spotted rooting for acorns around the island.

Chapter 1

Portrait of a nation

Drawing an orderly picture of Italianness is hard – and not just because it's a riotous country. From north to south, there are many different versions of national identity. Much of this is due to Italy's fragmented history: various invaders and monarchs left behind a stratified set of traditions that are still visible across the peninsula's culture, food and architecture. A staggeringly diverse landscape also plays its part: spend time among Alpine peaks in winter and lazily bobbing in the Mediterranean come summer and you would be forgiven for believing you had visited two separate countries. There are some common characteristics though – chiefly a dedication to community. A lifestyle revolving around togetherness is played out in stadiums, churches and on the streets – all of which act as theatres for the enthusiasm, passion and exuberance that Italians bring to the everyday.

SERVIZIO
BAR
GOLDEN

Summer:
Here comes the sun

Italy is a perfectly pleasant place year-round but it's during the summer that it turns into the nation conjured up by most people's imaginations. Italians pretty much own the concept of a long summer. Schools are shut from mid-June to mid-September, meaning that children enjoy virtually uninterrupted freedom for three months. But adults know how to take long breaks too: August is the "off" month par excellence, especially in the days surrounding *Ferragosto*, a public holiday that takes place on 15 August. For two to three weeks, the country shuts shop: companies stop operating while employees decamp to the beach. This nationwide labour halt may appear bizarre to outsiders but in Italy this tradition is observed obsessively. Cities become ghost towns while seaside resorts bustle (at a laid-back pace, of course).

In the waters of northeastern Sardinia, close to the town of Puntaldia, you're never far from an aperitivo. Whether you're lazing around on a pontoon or have found a secluded cove at which to drop anchor, the guys at Golden White will deliver homemade granita, gelato and fruit salad – or a spritz – to your deck.

High on the verdant hills of the Amalfi Coast, Positano appears like a vision when driving on the SS163, a panoramic stretch of road that hugs the cliffs and leads all the way to Sorrento. At the foot of the town, the Spiaggia Grande is one of the biggest beaches in the area.

In Forte dei Marmi, one of the country's upscale resorts, the sandy beach is neatly parcelled out between different *bagni*: at Orsa Maggiore, service is particularly attentive and each spot comes complete with loungers, chairs and towels.

Heineken

Though it is still blessed with wild, unspoilt beaches, much of Italian seaside life takes place at the *bagni*. These organised beach clubs cover a large portion of the coast in regions including Liguria, Tuscany, Veneto and Emilia-Romagna. They normally consist of a simple shack (which often doubles as a restaurant and bar), changing cabins and regimented rows of umbrellas and loungers. Most Italian families are habit-driven when it comes to holidaying and tend to return not only to the same *bagni* every year but to book the identical spot – which is how summertime friendships between umbrella neighbours form over the seasons.

BAGNI FIORE

Set in the bay of Paraggi, near the Ligurian town of Santa Margherita Ligure, the green umbrellas of Bagni Fiore seem to mirror the colour of the emerald waters of this small shore. Founded in 1927, the beach club extends from sand to its teak terrace.

Alongside the usual crime novels and crinkled newspapers, *La Settimana Enigmistica* is a weekly crosswords title often spotted under beach umbrellas. Founded in 1932 it remains one of country's most-sold magazines.

Restaurant Rada sits on Positano's main beach, its structure excavated out of the rock. Here customers can enjoy delectable lunches – from spaghetti with sea urchins to grilled *ricciola* (amberjack) and the fluffiest *torta caprese*.

Making gelato in Naples is a competitive business: as soon as the city's temperature rises, it becomes the most popular treat on the beach of Mergellina and also the scorching city streets. In the upmarket neighbourhood of Posillipo, Bilancione is recognised as one of the best *gelaterie* in town.

Service:
With a smile

For some, good service means a deferential attitude towards the customer but in Italy the practice tends to be slightly different. Of course patrons are polite but the main ingredient for great hospitality – or retail – is a friendliness that tends to put people on the same level. It is not uncommon for hoteliers, restaurateurs or shop owners to engage in long, tangential chats, and most are more than happy to provide personalised and honest advice. Service in Italy is about people's joy of sharing what they know they can do best: there's an understandable element of pride in recognising one's own skills, expertise and knowledge. The best way to enjoy it? Trust the house. They'll always bring out the best wine in the cellar.

Turin's Caffè Torino adopts the bull as its emblem: the animal appears above the bar but also as a brass plaque on the pavement in front of its entrance. Stepping on it is said to bring good luck (which is why the metal is so shiny).

Gio Ponti's design for the Hotel Parco dei Principi in Sorrento considered the most minute of details – including a reception desk covered in ceramic pebbles. The result perfectly frames the activity of the staff behind.

In Rome's Ghetto, Piperno is a restaurant where traditional and simple Roman-Jewish dishes are delivered with deference. The white-suited and bow-tie-wearing staff are almost as famous as the *carciofi alla giudia* on the menu.

The vast majority of hotels in Italy are independent businesses – and even the country's most successful hospitality groups tend to be small in size and retain plenty of personality. Pellicano Hotels is one such example: the group runs Ischia's Mezzatorre Hotel and gave it a revamp that has maintained the charm of the former watchtower.

For a hotel that can easily lay claim to being one of the best on the Amalfi Coast, the San Pietro di Positano is remarkably hidden away and unassuming. Much of this is due to the discretion of the Cinque family and the dedication of its staff, including waiter Fabio (*pictured, above*), who has seen through an impressive number of summer seasons.

Food:
On the menu

Italy is more than just a nation that's good at food, it is a nation that's obsessed with it: eating it, making it, producing it. Hardly a conversation goes by without a reference to a culinary feat, while eavesdropping on phone calls on the street often reveals people are either recounting their last meal or planning the next. The reason for this is that it's easy for everybody to eat well: excellent produce is available cheaply at the many food markets dotted around most neighbourhoods. The majority of recipes that have made Italian food famous – pasta in all its sauces, pizza with all its toppings, tomato-and-bread soups and salads – are, in fact, not only simple but also inexpensive to make, turning gastronomy into a democratic exercise in community-building.

The Taverna Blue Marlin in Sardinia's Porto Pino is little more than a trellis-covered shack, a stone's throw from a pristine beach and its marina. What comes out of the kitchen, though, is nothing short of spectacular: healthy portions of spaghetti with *vongole* and *bottarga* never last long on these tables.

Insalata di polpo (octopus salad) often includes chunks of boiled potato but sometimes you need nothing more than parsley, lemon, salt and pepper. The softness and juiciness of the meat belies more skill than you might think.

There's no fixed ingredients list for *fritto misto*, the staple of beach-side lunches: hidden under light, crispy batter you'll find whatever small catch was found in the fisherman's net that day.

Though you're welcome to seek out pristine establishments with starched tablecloths and elegant tableware, the vast majority of restaurants across Italy err on the unassuming side – and it's this accessible, popular vernacular that makes them all the more charming. All around the country, you'll find *trattorie* where the tables are covered in yellow paper mats, wine is served in large carafes and portions are unfailingly excessive. Most expand on the notion of homemade food turning it into a homely, comforting feast. Loud with chatter and animated by brisk (but never rude) service, these are places where people sit down for a proper meal of *antipasto*, *primo*, *secondo e dolce* – and where it's hard not to leave content.

FIORDILATTE
FRANCIA
0,79 L'ETTO
BUONI
PASTO
OK
PROSCIUTTO
COTTO
SENZA
POLIFOSFATI
0,99
L'ETTO
LEVISSIMA
Santagata
Negroni

The Mercato Nomentano, built in the 1920s, has been serving Rome's Trieste-Salario district for almost a century. Many of the stall owners took over from family, like Stefano Piergentili, whose stand sells wine and meat from Marche.

Italy's produce spans the spectrum of the warmest hues, is bold in flavour and bursting with juice. This bounty is ready to be put to use at the bed and breakfast Castello di Potentino on the slopes of Tuscany's Monte Amiata.

The Dolomites may not be the first place you'd expect to find a pasta producer but the waters of the area's pure springs contribute to Pasta Felicetti's crisp taste. Its spaghetti, which is made with high-quality, organic durum wheat, is left to dry slowly in the mountain air.

Not all parmesan warrants the title of Parmigiano-Reggiano. The designated denomination applies only to specific hard cheeses made in the provinces of Parma, Reggio Emilia and Modena (plus areas near Bologna and Mantua). Here, the large golden wheels are being left to mature for two years.

Vineyards can be spotted in Italy everywhere from high-altitude fields to the rolling hills of Piedmont, Tuscany and beyond – proving every terrain has a grape to match. Venissa, on the small island of Mazzorbo in the Venetian lagoon, has to be one of the most unique. Owner Gianluca Bisol decided to revive the lesser-known Dorona di Venezia variety to produce a prized white wine.

Faith:
From the heavens

Though it's much less common to find someone who goes to mass every Sunday than it once was, religion continues to shape the country's identity, politics and history. As the seat of the Catholic church, the Vatican has influenced Italian society and its customs for centuries. Much of the nation's widespread traditionalism owes its beginnings to the doctrine. Today, the Pope's opinion is respected and valued by governors and the governed alike – and crucifixes still adorn classrooms. While many may associate Catholicism with the pomp of great *palazzi* and majestically dressed cardinals, much of the church's activity is still carried out in local parishes that have long functioned as cornerstones of community. Despite the country's deep-rooted Christianity, it is also home to a significant Jewish population while recent migration is changing the nature of faith in Italy too.

For all the crowds on Venice's *calli* (streets), heading inside one of its many white marble churches often opens up a peaceful parallel universe where respectful silence reigns. Religious spaces often host the country's most awe-inspiring Renaissance masterpieces – such as Bellini's altarpiece inside San Zaccaria – which can be admired in contemplative peace and quiet.

The market for religious souvenirs is very active in Italy: there are 90 companies in the capital while nationwide sales are worth €30m annually. From rosaries to crosses, these objects end up in the homes of devout Catholics the world over.

The Swiss Guards were founded in 1506 to defend the then Pope (Julius II, also known as "the warrior Pope") during a time when political assassinations in Rome were rife. The division now includes 135 guards. Despite wearing a Renaissance-style uniform and brandishing a halberd, the guards are no antiquated group: they can also be equipped with more modern firearms.

Jorge Mario Bergoglio became Pope in 2013 under the name Francis and was the 266th to acquire this role. Each pope is elected by a conclave of cardinals who often deliberate in secret for days on end, voting as many as four times a day. If they haven't agreed on a name, they announce the failed resolution via black smoke from a chimney inside the Sistine Chapel. When they have chosen, the smoke becomes white. Here the Pope welcomes Sir Rodney Williams, governor-general of Antigua and Barbuda, to the Holy See.

APOSTOLO
PRINCEPS PAMPHILIVS
INNOCENTII X FRATRIS
A FVNDAMENTIS

Before the Second World War, Trieste was home to a large Jewish community, which is why the city's synagogue remains one of the biggest in Europe. Completed in 1912 to a plan by architects Ruggero and Arduino Berlam, it was intended to replace four smaller temples. With its golden mosaic, it is an impressive space with embellishments inspired by the Middle East.

Spaces: *Gather round*

Maybe it's because Italy is a country that's blessed with sunshine for many months of the year that so much of life is spent outside. But not only that: ever since ancient Roman times, cities were built to encourage conversation outdoors. Today the *piazza* is perhaps the most important building block of an Italian city. In itself, it is nothing more than a paved space surrounded by buildings – but as the seat of commercial, religious and political goings-on, it has always been much more than a large thoroughfare. Much may have changed since the times of Rome's "forum" but architecture in Italy has kept a close link to its civic, public purpose.

Though it now includes structures built through the ages, the history of the Roman Forum begins in the 6th century when a swamp was drained to become the centre of public life. The ruins of the Temple of Saturn and the Arch of Septimius Severus can be seen here.

The national conversation around fascist-era architecture has always been thorny. Many institutional buildings such as Rome's Palazzo della Civiltà Italiana – better known as "Colosseo Quadrato" – still stand. Italian Rationalism, as the style is known, was deliberately used to promote fascist ideology but it is now being re-evaluated (and is sometimes understood as a historical memento).

Plenty of Roman architecture has stood the test of time and among the best preserved is the Pantheon in Rome. Its perfect proportions (the domed structure was built so it could contain an imaginary sphere) went on to influence many other works and shape the aesthetics of neoclassicism.

The Benetton empire has its creative heart in the Veneto town of Catena di Villorba. It's here that Luciano Benetton and Oliviero Toscani asked Japanese architect Tadao Ando in 1994 to refit the 17th-century Villa Pastega Manera. The building is now home to Fabrica: a creative research centre offering residencies in everything from photography and music to design for under-25s.

Having visited the Foreign Ministry in Brasilia, publisher Giorgio Mondadori decided he'd only be content with architect Oscar Niemeyer designing a new HQ for his burgeoning business. The building, set on the outskirts of Milan in the town of Segrate, was completed in 1975 and became Niemeyer's favourite project in Europe.

The Carlo Mollino-designed theatre hall at Turin's Teatro Regio is shaped like a shell. It can host 1,582 people in its red velvet stalls while 31 opulent boxes line the auditorium. The space is lit by a chandelier made up of 1,762 aluminium tubes and 1,900 Perspex sticks.

In Venice's Piazza San Marco, under the storied porticoes, is this unexpected corner of modernism. Designed by Carlo Scarpa, the showroom for electronics firm Olivetti was commissioned to match the technology held within. The space is dominated by a bold (yet apparently floating) staircase. Palazzo Azzurro in Turin (*right*) – better known as Palazzo degli Oblò – brings a touch of experimentation to Corso Francia.

Both constructed in the 1950s, the apartments on Via Vigoni 13 (*left*) and the shopping arcade Galleria Strasburgo (*above*) are only two of the many works realised by architect and urbanist Luigi Caccia Dominioni in his home city of Milan.

Much like the outside of Mondadori's HQ, the interior – also designed by Niemeyer – was just as pioneering: it was an early proponent for open-plan space and intended to foster collaboration. As well as five floors of offices, the structure includes an auditorium, library and canteen.

PANSA
INTERNI
PANORAMA
PROMETEO
CASABELLA
TERRA
MILANO

Teatro Regio creator Carlo Mollino was famously eccentric – which is why Casa Mollino on Turin's Via Napione is filled with extravagant touches, including references to ancient Egypt and symbolic rebirth. Used as a secret refuge rather than a residence, the mysterious house is now a museum.

The reconstruction flurry that followed the Second World War brought with it plenty of *palazzine* (apartment blocks). Today, most city-dwellers inhabit flats, often accessed via attractive lobbies. The block on Milan's Corso Italia (*this page*) features mosaics by Francesco Somaini.

THE UNION
OF FIRE
AND WATER
ALILAGUNA

Getting around:
On the go

If there's one thing you need in order to move efficiently in Italy, it's agility: the best vehicles are small, zippy ones that allow you to zoom through traffic (be it on land or water). Though dexterity is needed on the streets – and to park – this is also a country of impressive infrastructure, from huge ships to historical roads.

In Venice you need only hail one of the many water taxis navigating the canals for a thrilling panoramic excursion. On Lake Como (*above*) you can rent your own speedboat – though there are also kayaks for those after a slower pace.

With more than 18 million vehicles produced since its 1946 launch, Piaggio's Vespa is more than just a means of transport. A cultural icon for the country, the scooter has been immortalised by a number of artistic representations from films such as *La Dolce Vita* and *Caro Diario* to Lunapop's 1990s hit "50 Special".

In Europe, Italy benefits the most from the cruise-ship industry in terms of employment and turnover (though the presence of large boats in the Venice basin is a constant controversy). Most depart from the Ligurian ports of Genoa and Savona, though some worldwide voyages leave from just outside Rome.

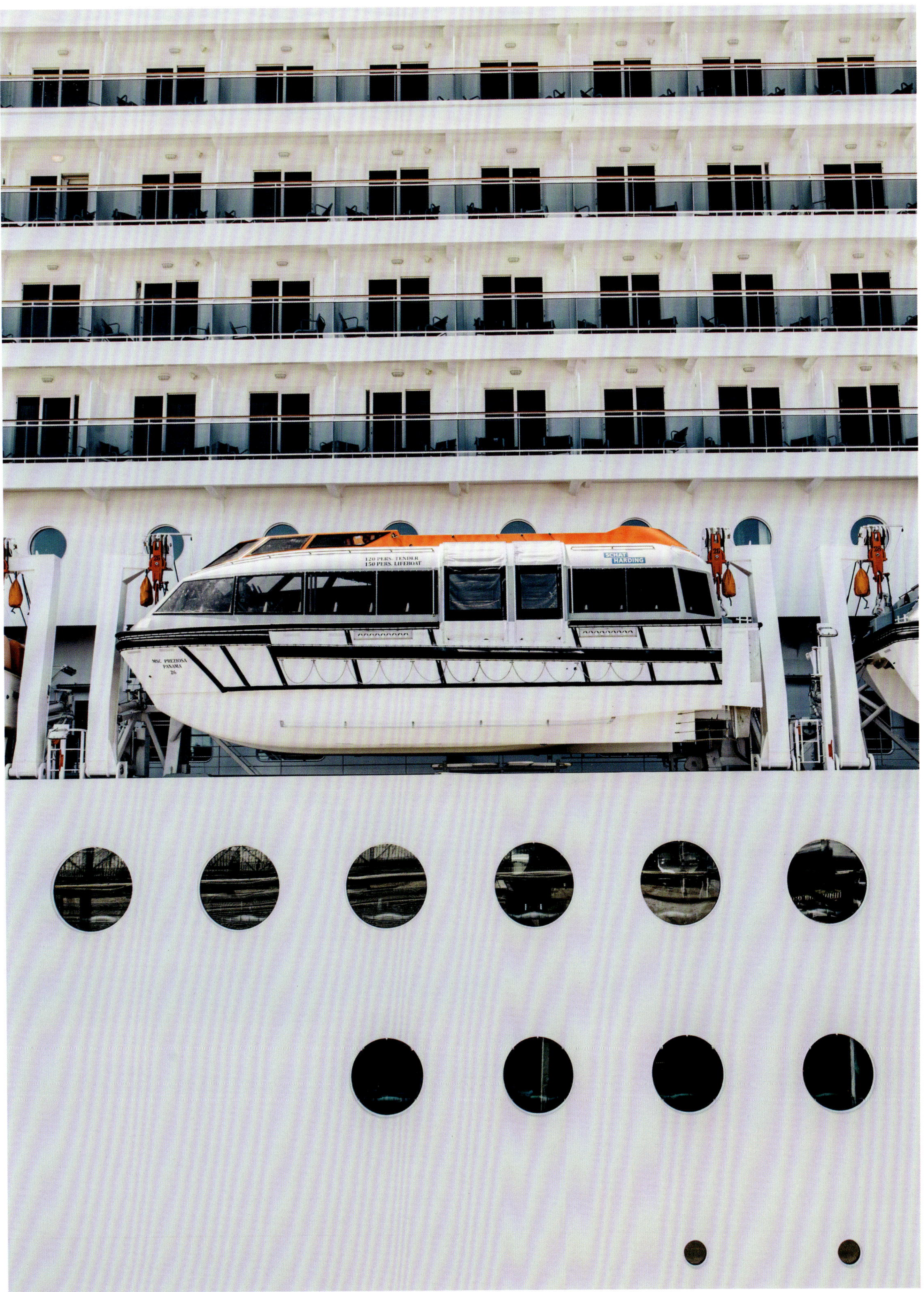
120 PERS. TENDER
150 PERS. LIFEBOAT
SCHAT
HARDING
MSC PREZIOSA
PANAMA
26

The nation's high-speed train fleet includes the Frecciarossa 1000 as its most modern model. Designed by Turinese studio Bertone and built by Hitachi Rail Italy and Bombardier, it is Europe's fastest train.

Plenty of architectural and urban inventions can be attributed to ancient Rome – including roads. Built using an innovative system of stone laying to connect the capital to its provinces, they were key to the Empire's trade and military success. Some of the historical routes have been transformed into the motorways that criss-cross the nation today.

Landscape: *Scene change*

The postcard-perfect image of Italy often consists of rolling hills topped with pointy cypress trees or colourful, red-roofed homes clinging to cliffsides. Though the snowy tips of the Alps are just as Italian as the pristine bays of the Med, there's one thing that much of the landscape in this country shares: even the wildest spots are never too far from a town.

This densely populated land has made the most of its ability to coexist with nature, however extreme, so much so that you'll find villages and cities even at the feet of active volcanoes. Still, you would perhaps be surprised to find Italy's plentiful wildlife – from brown bears to wolves and ibex – has found ways to survive in its forests and mountains too.

Though there are many large lakes scattered across northern Italy, Como is arguably the most popular. A spin on the water in a sleek runabout is the best (and most exciting) way to take in the stunning surroundings.

Hugging the whole of northern Italy with their white peaks, the Italian Alps trace the confines of Valle d'Aosta, Piedmont, Lombardy, Veneto, Trentino-Alto Adige and Friuli Venezia Giulia – where influences from across the border often manage to climb over the mountains.

A lot of Italy's terrain – particularly its fertile hills – is used for agriculture. The sector employs around a million people and is increasingly attracting young, ambitious entrepreneurs unwilling to let rural traditions die. Much is organic and high-quality – as testified by the many denominations for produce.

Due to its location on top of a major fault line, Italy is particularly prone to earthquakes and volcanic eruptions. Most of the country's peaks lie dormant though there are two that erupt frequently. Of those, Etna, on Sicily's eastern coast, is the biggest (and at 3,300m, the tallest in Europe). Its summit is often surrounded by pillows of smoke – even when it's covered with a layer of snow.

Uniforms:
Suited and booted

Many Italian corps look like they've come from another era. Their uniforms are often based on old-school, shoulder-heavy suits and extravagant headgear. These outfits work by asserting the authority of elegance rather than a more obvious intimidation – and they appear very impressive at gatherings and parades.

Founded in 1872, the Alpini (*left*) are the Italian army's mountain division – the world's oldest of such – created to defend against France and the Habsburg Empire. They still wear their characteristic felt hat, topped by a raven's feather. The Corpo Forestale (*above*) also works at altitude, protecting the wilderness.

Marching bands are a common feature of town fairs and celebrations for institutional or religious events. This one, captured during a hot Sicilian summer, is a performance work by multidisciplinary artist Marinella Senatore as part of contemporary biennial Manifesta, in homage to the traditional parade.

Each of the many police units in Italy can be distinguished via its uniform. The Polizia Municipale officers (*left*) can be spotted by their elegant white hats, while the Bersaglieri (*above*) – a specialised infantry division – wear a wide-brimmed number with a cascade of black rooster feathers.

The Carabinieri, not to be mistaken for the standard police, are part of the Italian army and respond to the Ministry of Defence. Here their band – with members kitted out in their trademark black-and-red suits – perform at the French Embassy in Rome.

They may not be tasked with maintaining public order but train staff for state-owned Trenitalia take their uniforms very seriously too: inside stations and onboard they wear a well-cut suit with red neckerchief or tie – and can be identified thanks to a nameplate that gives a friendly touch.

Considering the nation's many car manufacturers, it is perhaps no surprise that its armed forces are equipped with some pretty impressive motors. While the Carabinieri's most common vehicle is an Alfa Romeo 159, the fastest car in their garage is an Alfa Romeo Giulia Quadrifoglio, which can reach speeds of 307km/h.

The first Italian scout groups were founded in 1910 and, nowadays, the vast majority are joined in the Agesci organisation, which has a strong Catholic identity. Today, there are about 220,000 scouts in Italy: the little pack portrayed here in a park in Rome bears the organisation's wolf insignia which, incidentally, is also the city's own.

Style:
A look to last

Italy's fashion industry traverses a wide gamut, from the most prestigious, world-famous brands to a tight-knit network of small companies, textile producers and high-end manufacturers. Most importantly, this is a country that cares about its looks, and knows how to recognise a good cut and well-made materials. Above all, Italian style is about bold choices and time-honoured classics that last a lifetime, with some extravagant details added in for good measure.

Though it also includes a men's version, Milan Fashion Week is at its dazzling best during its womenswear events. Around 70 runway shows and 90 presentations take place twice a year throughout the city.

Around the country, there are plenty of purveyors who ensure the most traditional trimmings of menswear are kept alive and well – but brands including Barena Venezia (*left*) are also hard at work rethinking tailoring in a contemporary and comfortable version that still delivers on elegance.

When it comes to fashion, fearless is the word – plunging necklines, high heels, fur and statement colours all feature heavily – and every occasion is worth dressing up for. Party-goers at the French Embassy in Rome (*above*) show how to wear clothes with confidence, while Cellina von Mannstein (*right*) of Forst brewery exudes her singular flair.

Breezy, everyday elegance doesn't need many trimmings: a linen suit, good shirt or sharply cut coat will do the job. Textures and fabrics are of the utmost importance.

Di Bartolomei

area pedonale
eccetto veicoli diretti aree interne ai fabbricati
FENDI

Some Italian boutiques are nothing short of palatial. In 2016, Fendi re-fitted this building not far from the Spanish Steps in Rome and transformed it into a glitzy shop-cum-hotel (which also comprises a workshop).

This prized shop by leatherware specialist Tod's is on Via Montenapoleone, Milan's main artery of luxury retail. The street may be less than 500m long but you'll find a cluster of brands, from Ermenegildo Zegna to Loro Piana and Gucci, all well-tailored elbow to elbow with one another.

Prada's Milan outpost in the Galleria Vittorio Emanuele II is the brand's original and still retains fittings from when it opened in 1913. The location is so important to the company that it contributed (in collaboration with Versace) to a restoration of the glass-topped arcade in 2014. The historical digs of Neapolitan tie-maker E. Marinella on Via Riviera di Chiaia (*right*) may be small but its products are stocked around the world.

E. MARINELLA
Shirtmaker
Outfitter
E. MARINELLA

Trade fairs:
Show and sell

Many countries organise trade events but in Italy they are particularly popular and well-attended. Far from being circumscribed to soulless exhibition centres, plenty of fairs spill into the cities that host them, turning into joyous events suffused with a sense of celebration rather than just cold business dealings. Being home to so many high-end specialised manufacturers has consecrated Italy as the prime meeting point for both the design and fashion industries: these expert salespeople really know how to pitch themselves to an international audience.

Half the fun of attending Pitti Uomo, Italy's most important trade fair dedicated to menswear, is admiring the so-called "peacocks" that parade in front of the Fortezza da Basso grounds. For buyers that travel here from all over the world, starch and shoe polish are never spared.

Alestalo × Judin × Väre
Lassi Alestalo
www.lassialestalo.com
@designlassialestalo
@hnrjdn
Laura Väre
www.lauravare.com
@lauravre

From Australia to Uruguay, every designer's ambition is to showcase a creation at Milan's Salone del Mobile. No other appointment on the design calendar compares. Around 2,300 companies take up a stall inside the sprawling grounds of Fiera Rho, often building ambitious displays, while hundreds of presentations take place across the city in the Fuorisalone – meaning most people struggle to even scratch the surface of what's available over the week's shenanigans.

Venice's Arsenale and Giardini areas are home to the pavilions that host the city's Biennale, a cultural festival which alternates between an art and architecture focus each year. Twenty-nine nations have their own permanent spaces; the months-long exhibitions are a time for experimenting with avant-garde ideas that set the tone in their disciplines.

From fashion to food and design to beach clubs, Italians have put their stamp on a myriad sectors. They have managed to market and sell an entire way of life worldwide – flying the flag for Italy Inc in the process.

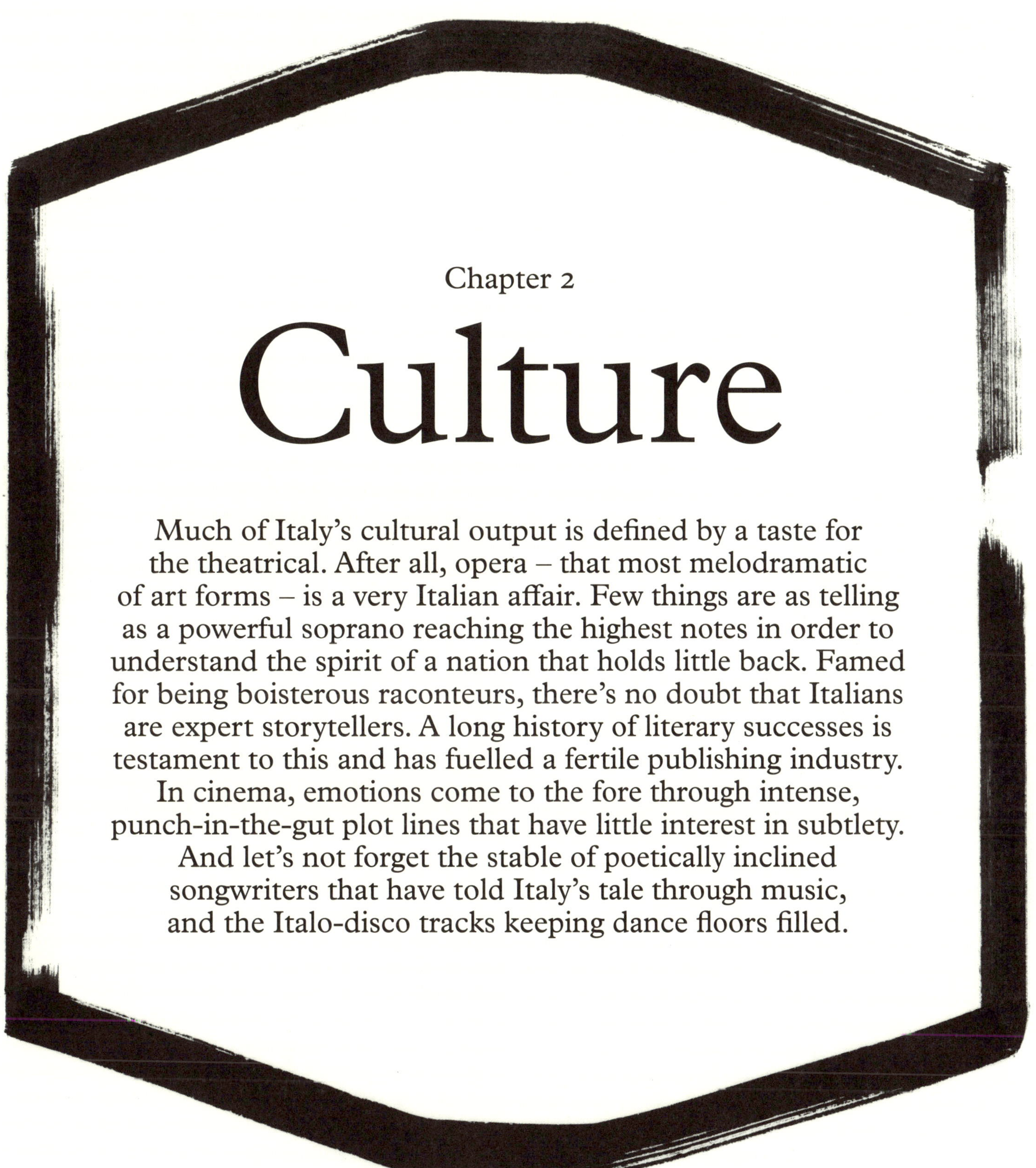

Chapter 2

Culture

Much of Italy's cultural output is defined by a taste for the theatrical. After all, opera – that most melodramatic of art forms – is a very Italian affair. Few things are as telling as a powerful soprano reaching the highest notes in order to understand the spirit of a nation that holds little back. Famed for being boisterous raconteurs, there's no doubt that Italians are expert storytellers. A long history of literary successes is testament to this and has fuelled a fertile publishing industry. In cinema, emotions come to the fore through intense, punch-in-the-gut plot lines that have little interest in subtlety. And let's not forget the stable of poetically inclined songwriters that have told Italy's tale through music, and the Italo-disco tracks keeping dance floors filled.

Museums:
On display

There are enough Renaissance wonders in Italy's world-famous museums to keep you occupied for years but the country's artistic bounty extends beyond marble statues and frescoes. From cutting-edge installations to arresting architecture and inventive ways to display archaeological finds, here's our pick of an illustrious bunch of cultural institutions.

Fondazione Prada
Milan

With a permanent collection comprising works by Louise Bourgeois and Jeff Koons, and an events programme offering everything from fashion shows to philosophy conferences, Fondazione Prada is Milan's – and possibly the country's – leading contemporary arts and culture venue. Its temporary exhibitions have seen Steve McQueen's first Italian show and performance art from choreographer Billy Cowie but many visitors come for the architecture alone.

The fashion giant's cultural foundation was set up in 1995 in a smaller exhibition space and two decades later moved into its Rem Koolhaas-designed headquarters on the city's southern fringes – which is now enjoying something of a shake up thanks to its arrival.

The venue encompasses vast swathes of gallery-space spread between old distillery buildings, a concrete tower and so-called "haunted house" (dating back to the 1910s), the exterior of which is gilded in 24-carat gold leaf. Koolhaas also added a mirror-clad cinema building where current arthouse releases, cult classics and specially curated series from the likes of Pedro Almodóvar and Damien Hirst are screened. Another draw is the Wes Anderson-designed café Bar Luce (*see page 226*).

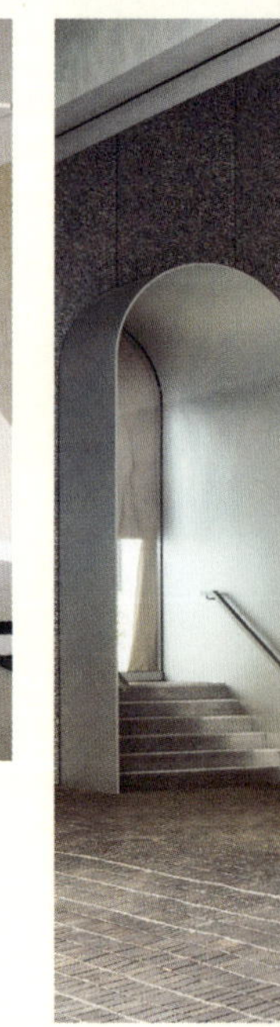

Centrale Montemartini
Rome

Powers both ancient and modern meet in this old electricity plant, where statues of Roman gods and emperors stand among vast machinery. Housed in Rome's former Giovanni Montemartini thermoelectric centre, the museum is located in the Ostiense-Marconi industrial complex on the River Tiber.

Inaugurated in 1912 and shut down in the early 1960s, the plant is a temple to state enterprise combining grandeur and parochial pride with lofty interiors. But its use as a museum was never intended to be permanent. Sculptures were transferred from the Musei Capitolini while it underwent works in 1997 with the plant hosting a temporary exhibition, "Machines and Gods", that placed ancient marble incarnations of deities among fascist-era steam turbines, diesel engines and air canisters.

The exhibition proved so popular that it was decided Centrale Montemartini should become a permanent home for a collection of the Musei Capitolini's most recent acquisitions. Alongside Greek and Roman sculptures, Pope Pius IX's grand papal train from 1858 is on display while the museum's "From Myth to Miracle" exhibition comprises a series of Roman sarcophagi.

Address to impress
Come fashion week, plenty of Milan's cultural venues play host to runway shows and presentations. Among them is the fascinating Villa Necchi Campiglio – a gorgeous 1930s residence which was immortalised in Luca Guadagnino's 2009 film *I Am Love*.

Messner Mountain Museum
South Tyrol

In mountaineering circles, no name commands more respect than that of climber Reinhold Messner. This museum in his native South Tyrol is a celebration of not just his life and achievements – of which there are many – but the mountains themselves and those who live among them.

The museum was born in 1995 when Messner opened his summer residence, a medieval castle in the Vinschgau Valley, to the public. He has since launched five more sites across the Dolomites including another converted castle which hosts exhibitions exploring the lives of high-altitude communities. "I'm interested in telling stories about man and the mountains," says Messner. "Human beings have lived and survived for 10,000 years in them."

The museum's latest outpost opened in 2015 in the Kronplatz ski resort and is housed in a Zaha Hadid-designed bunker atop a 2,275m mountain peak (*pictured*). Its subterranean exhibition space is dedicated to the story of modern mountaineering and offers impressive glass viewing platforms that jut out of the rock to reveal sweeping vistas of the surrounding Alpine peaks.

Uffizi
Florence

Virtually everyone who visits Italy makes peace with the idea of long queues for museums, but if you only have time to wait for one, make it the Uffizi. The palatial Giorgio Vasari-designed building was commissioned in the 1560s by Cosimo I de' Medici to house his offices or *uffizi* (hence the name). Never intended as a museum, it acted as a private gallery for the Medici family – and subsequently the Habsburg-Lorraines – filled with their rare and treasured artworks. It wasn't until 1769 that the Uffizi was opened to the public.

A work of art in its own right, with impressive frescoed ceilings and ornate tiled flooring, the space comprises 93 rooms bedecked with 13th to 18th-century artworks as well as a library holding thousands of books and precious manuscripts.

Some of the most famous paintings in the world adorn the walls of this historic museum, from "Venus of Urbino" by Titian and "Doni Tondo" by Michelangelo to Leonardo Da Vinci's "Annunciation" and Fra Angelico's "Coronation of the Virgin". But the room that draws the most crowds? The one that is home to Botticelli's "Birth of Venus". The Uffizi is deservedly the hottest ticket in a town full of blockbusters.

Museo Archeologico Regionale Antonino Salinas
Palermo

There are countless (often fairly stuffy) archaeology museums across Italy but the Museo Archeologico Regionale Antonino Salinas is a particular joy to visit, not just for the artefacts but for the building that houses it. Located in the former Oratory of Saint Philip Neri, its two courtyards, complete with restored marble columns and majolica tiles, are where the museum sets itself apart from the rest. Filled with exotic and exuberant plants – including bananas – one of the squares is home to a 16th-century fountain where you'll find a bale of sleepy turtles.

Among the plentiful relics to be found in the exhibition halls – many of which were discovered by the museum's namesake, Palermo-born archaeologist Antonino Salinas – is one of its most notable exhibits: a reconstruction of a Greek temple frieze.

Remains of the day
Occasionally, Roman ruins get a bad rap from those who've been disappointed by visits to archaeological sites, finding little more than a pile of rubble. But Pompeii and Herculaneum – just a (volcanic) stone's throw from Naples – never fail to impress. The ancient cities were preserved almost entirely intact after Mount Vesuvius erupted in 79AD covering them in a thick layer of ashes. Today they are deservedly two of the most visited cultural sites in the country.

Art galleries: *Watch this space*

With plenty of pristine *palazzi* to take over and fill with edgy work, many commercial galleries in Italy have redefined the idea of the white cube. Courtyards and grand apartments provide a stimulating contrast for the contemporary art that hangs on their walls.

Galleria Lorcan O'Neill
Rome

Though it may not be considered the art capital of the world, or even Italy, Rome is still attracting top talent from across the border. But why are creatives choosing to relocate? Perhaps it could have something to do with the city's relaxed approach to both art and life.

One such professional is Irish curator Lorcan O'Neill (*pictured*). "I always liked Rome. I used to come and visit Cy Twombly and a day's work would turn into a few days' stay," says O'Neill. "It was a good opportunity to be independent, work with artists I admired and do something that counted – I don't think I could have dented London's art scene in the same way."

O'Neill opened his first gallery in Rome's Trastevere in 2003 and moved into the old stables of the 17th-century Palazzo Santa Croce in 2014. Visitors are greeted by the huge fountain in the courtyard, followed by a plate-glass door that leads into a barn of a room with eight-metre-high ceilings. The space is essentially a white cube, subtly saved from looking ascetic by the vaulted ceilings on high and traditional terracotta floor. Though small, it represents some of the biggest names in contemporary art from Tracey Emin, Anselm Kiefer and Richard Long to Italians such as Luigi Ontani.

Galleria Continua
Rome & San Gimignano

Founded in the unlikely location of the Tuscan hill town San Gimignano, Galleria Continua's mission is to "help contemporary art expand beyond its typical confines," says Maurizio Rigillo, who opened the gallery with Mario Cristiani and Lorenzo Fiaschi in 1990. The trio has shown contemporary artists in villages across Italy, including a Carsten Höller carousel on a rural hill in Basilicata. "That's the spirit we were born with," explains Rigillo, "to make art available to a wider public, so someone might happen upon it and form a relationship with it."

The gallery has grown into a renowned space with an international presence, attracting heavyweights such as Anish Kapoor, Antony Gormley, Mona Hatoum and Michelangelo Pistoletto. The San Gimignano gallery covers a former cinema, stone tower and several more sites. Locations have opened in other unexpected spots: Beijing, Havana, a countryside mill outside Paris and in Rome's St Regis hotel.

Rome is hardly virgin territory for galleries, says Rigillo, but beyond exhibition rooms, the artists have free rein to place works throughout the St Regis's lobby and bar, seating strange figures next to patrons. "We like to surprise people with art," he says.

Massimo de Carlo
Milan

Since 1987, Massimo de Carlo has been bringing both rising and established international stars to Milan. De Carlo, who is one of Italy's most powerful art dealers, was responsible for introducing the likes of John Armleder and Carsten Höller to Italian audiences and catapulted homegrown talent including Alighiero Boetti and Maurizio Cattelan onto the global stage.

The gallery encompasses premises in London, Hong Kong and a Kengo Kuma-designed space in Paris as well as two addresses in De Carlo's native Milan. One is housed beneath the elaborate ceilings of the Palazzo Belgioioso (*pictured*) designed in the late 1700s by architect Giuseppe Piermarini – best known for the Teatro alla Scala (*see page 148*).

The gallery moved into its new headquarters and second Milanese space in 2019, occupying a floor of the historic Casa Corbellini-Wassermann. This former 1930s apartment block lay empty for 15 years before De Carlo snapped it up and enlisted Studio Binocle to reinvigorate its interiors. The result is a refined eight-room gallery complete with striped Ornavasso marble flooring that has since hosted artists such as Gianfranco Baruchello and Marisa Merz.

Film:
Action packed

Ever since the golden era of Cinecittà, Italy has had a healthy homegrown cinema scene that's kept its screens flickering with anything from light-hearted comedies, weighty neorealist dramas and gorgeous arthouse films. A new generation of directors is winning Oscars and reviving fortunes abroad – but at home, audiences have always been keen on independent, local productions.

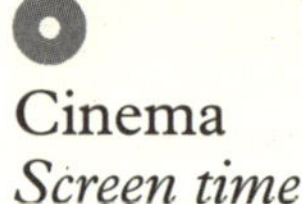

Cinema
Screen time

Director Giuseppe Tornatore's *Cinema Paradiso* paints a picture of an Italian screening room as an extension of the town square: a place where people meet, discuss (often loudly) and fall in love. While the rise of the multiplex, combined with the arrival of streaming services, may have made life harder for the independents, it's precisely that sense of community and service to the neighbourhood that has kept so many cinemas going across the peninsula.

Rather surprisingly, the number of tickets sold over the past two decades in the country has remained relatively stable: small cinemas in small towns have guaranteed a lifeline for many rural areas that would otherwise be cut-off from the release calendar. Some of these grassroots institutions have their own buildings, sometimes they are housed inside the local chapel: the Church still manages about 800 screens across Italy, in something of a throwback to its role as a social aggregator for many villages (and exercising, perhaps unexpectedly, little censorship on the programming).

Still, cinemas are at their best in their community role when set up outdoors: in Rome an organisation of young cinephiles, I Ragazzi del Cinema America, runs alfresco screenings so well-loved that prime minister Giuseppe Conte has been seen sitting cross-legged on a blanket. Director Nanni Moretti runs his own arthouse cinema, Nuovo Sacher, from inside a former fascist-era social club in the capital. And every summer, beaches, promenades and ancient castles turn into open-air settings for (often free) film festivals.

Italy on film

1.
Ladri di Biciclette (1948)
Vittorio De Sica
A neorealist classic, De Sica's *Ladri di Biciclette* (Bicycle Thieves) is a portrait of poverty in postwar Rome. It follows protagonist Antonio Ricci on a hunt around the city in search of his stolen set of wheels.

2.
L'Avventura (1960)
Michelangelo Antonioni
A group of friends on a boat trip around the Aeolian Islands have their holiday drawn to a dramatic halt when one of their party goes missing. This masterful drama features a particularly haunting performance from Monica Vitti.

3.
Caro Diario (1993)
Nanni Moretti
Italy's answer to Woody Allen, director Moretti stars in his Palme d'Or nominated comedy. Semi-autobiographical, the movie is structured like the pages of an open diary and tracks Moretti's day-to-day, including riding his Vespa through the streets of Rome.

4.
Gomorra (2008)
Matteo Garrone
This gritty drama is an unflinching study of mob rule in the impoverished fringes of Naples. Director Garrone used non-professional actors from the featured estates for many of the characters, giving the film a striking sense of realism.

5.
La Grande Bellezza (2013)
Paolo Sorrentino
An explosive critique of Italy's wealthy elite, this Oscar-winner tells the story of an ageing socialite at the centre of Rome's decadent nightlife. It's a visually sumptuous but melancholic piece of film-making from Sorrentino (*see page 200*) full of bacchanalian party scenes.

Cinecittà
Rome

Located on the outskirts of Rome, in an expansive lot, is the home of Italy's cinema industry. Opened in 1937, the Cinecittà studios were part of Mussolini's drive to equip the fascist regime with an expanded infrastructure for Italy's ailing film industry and the production of state propaganda. But it was the 1950s that saw the studios' heyday with dozens of Oscar-winning movies shot there – it is where Fellini made many of his features – as well as US films *Roman Holiday* and *Ben-Hur*, for which it earned the nickname "Hollywood on the Tiber".

After falling into decline in the late 20th century, the studios have seen a resurgence thanks to TV and its latest plot twist involves Netflix expressing an interest. Watch this space.

Spaghetti Western
It may seem counter-intuitive that in the 1960s and 1970s Italian directors became world-famous for films about the Wild West but the success of Sergio Leone's *A Fistful of Dollars* (and its Ennio Morricone soundtrack) spawned plenty of imitators – and a whole genre in itself. Spaghetti Westerns were more hot-blooded and violent than their American counterparts, often featuring more complex characters and sardonic humour. Much of the – ahem – shooting took place in southern Spain and Italy's dry plains, and sometimes in the Cinecittà studios. Despite relatively small budgets, films such as Sergio Corbucci's *Django* enjoyed huge popularity – and went on to inspire the likes of Quentin Tarantino.

Q&A
Alice Rohrwacher

With a strong domestic scene, Italy has never been short of films for its internal market – but not all of these creatives have managed to make their mark abroad. Film-maker Alice Rohrwacher, one of the brightest lights in the picture, is breaking that mould. Twice a winner at the Cannes Film Festival – *The Wonders* took home the Grand Prix in 2014 and *Lazzaro Felice* garnered Best Screenplay in 2018 – Rohrwacher's *Omelia Contadina*, a short she wrote and directed in collaboration with artist JR, is a pastoral elegy to her beloved Tuscan countryside. In Italy, even film is a family affair and her features have starred her sister, actress Alba Rohrwacher.

Why does the Italian countryside make such a presence in your films?
As a child, I lived in a rural commune in Tuscany, then my parents wanted to create their own world so we moved to a country house where my father raised bees. That was the inspiration for *The Wonders*, but it's not autobiographical. I don't want to make stories about individuals. I make collective stories – about problems that are part of everyone's lives. The land and what we're losing now is a problem for us all.

How did you decide to blend the Italian strains of neorealism and Fellini-esque magical realism?
There's a fluid relationship between what's real and fantastical. That's how I've always seen the world. It's not about what has happened in cinema before or what I think cinema should become. It's about telling the tales that make me fall in love with them, so it's a very personal thing. It's my vision.

What are the challenges of working in Italian cinema when there are so few female directors?
You should never turn difficulty into your banner. It should remain your secret and make you stronger, hungrier to succeed. In Italy, cinema is a world that's developed around men, around their desires and their visions but that, in my opinion, should make more women want to break into film-making. An underrepresented minority's point of view is always fascinating.

Does the collaboration with your sister affect your film-making?
Working with Alba is like working with a light – illuminating and occasionally blinding. Maybe I'm biased but I think she's the best actress in the world and to work with someone who knows you so well helps bring out the profound and personal elements of a project. Making a film together, you get to know each other deeply, even more so than as sisters. I'm very grateful we're so united in work and life.

Media:
What's new?

Italians are an opinionated bunch and they have developed mouthpieces to match their enthusiasm. Political goings-on are scrutinised and discussed by an ever-observant audience that enjoys engaging with the latest news. With well-stocked *edicole* (news kiosks) dotting the country as patrons of print, plenty of publications still sit proudly on the shelves.

National newspapers
The fine print

A quick scan reveals that Italy is still hungry for print, as national, regional and local dailies occupy a sizable chunk of the newsstand. Proudly partisan left, centrist and right-leaning titles – including papers affiliated with the Catholic Church – vie for attention, at times enticing readers with sales-boosting inserts on specific topics.

The general-interest national dailies that dominate the media landscape include Rome-based **1.** *La Repubblica*. Its attractive graphic design and liberal stance enjoys a large following and is bolstered by its popular collection of weekly pullouts such as style magazine *D* and culture-focused Sunday supplement *Robinson*. Milan-based **2.** *Corriere della Sera*, meanwhile, is the country's best-selling broadsheet and is more conservative in tone. Founded in 1876, it regularly features opinion pieces from leading commentators in the fields of economics, politics and culture.

Popular in its hometown of Turin, **3.** *La Stampa* has a more centrist stance while upstart **4.** *Domani* – launched in 2020 – is politically independent and progressive in outlook. At just 20 pages long, the modern, pared-back title reports from its spot in the Italian capital.

Those who want to follow the markets and business-oriented types turn to respected daily **5.** *Il Sole 24 Ore* for its exhaustive financial coverage. It also houses a popular radio station and circulates a much anticipated annual survey that ranks the quality of life in Italian cities and towns. Not surprisingly, the football-crazed country has three national sports dailies and Milan-based **6.** *La Gazzetta dello Sport* sits at the top of the heap thanks to its insightful match analysis.

La Repubblica
One of the country's leading dailies, *La Repubblica* has been unconventional since the get-go. When it opened in 1976, it found a loyal readership with its adversarial, left-leaning style. And over the last few years, thanks to art director Angelo Rinaldi and designer Francesco Franchi, the paper has undergone a number of interesting redesigns as well as the launch of vintage-looking culture supplement *Robinson*. As many publishers go digital, *La Repubblica* is backing print – though a concentrated version of what it was before: "Paper may be niche but it is still authoritative. When you see something in print it carries weight. People take notice," says Rinaldi.

Magazines
Just your type

Stellar graphic design, first-rate photography and sharp commentary keep readers coming back to print institutions time and again. Titles range from architectural bible *Domus*, founded in the 1920s by Gio Ponti, and fashion trailblazer *Vogue Italia* to culinary monthly *La Cucina Italiana*, which focuses on recipes and the country's wealth of gastronomic delights. Relative newcomers to the scene include men's style and fashion title *Icon*, quarterly *Studio*, with its mix of affairs and lifestyle coverage, and bimonthly *Undici* with its high-brow take on sports. Indie titles such as *Dispensa* and *Cartography* have also garnered success abroad.

Radio
Listen up

Playing the latest local pop and chart-topping artists, with backing vocals from a set of live programmes covering current events and culture, Italy's airwaves are a lively mix. Mid-mornings with *W l'Italia* from RTL 102.5 feature the stories both big and small dominating the headlines with engaging participation from listeners, while Radio Deejay's AM show *Deejay Chiama Italia* includes an animated roster of guests. Weekday afternoons see state-run network RAI air *Un giorno da pecora*, which regularly brings in politicians to comment on the day's events. Lastly, financial paper *Il Sole 24 Ore* boasts a loyal following for its radio channel, with a production that exceeds market coverage and includes the snarky evening talk show *La Zanzara*.

TV talk shows
Given a predisposition towards heated debate, Italians love to congregate around the TV to hear dynamic discussions. Broadcasters La7, Medlaset and state-run RAI offer the lion's share of programmes. The most storied of the crop includes week-night chat show *Porta a Porta*, an institution fronted by the indefatigable Bruno Vespa. *Otto e mezzo* and *Dimartedì* are among the most watched political talk shows where the public is guaranteed an uncompromised grilling and a fiery exchange of views thanks to their unflinching hosts, journalists Lilli Gruber (*see page 197*) and Giovanni Floris respectively. At the weekend, *Che tempo che fa* offers a more informal format with one-on-one interviews with prominent figures and celebrities from Italy and beyond, as well as a healthy dose of satire.

Opera:
Know the score

The over-the-top, sonorous fanfare of opera is a powerful cultural export. The fact that even foreign composers of arias have historically written their pieces to be belted out in Italian is proof of how intrinsically linked to the country this emotional art form is.

Teatro Regio
Turin

When stepping through the doors of the Teatro Regio's 1740s façade, a mid-century glass-fronted structure is not the first thing you'd expect to find. But that is exactly what awaits visitors to this historical yet unashamedly modern venue in Turin.

After a fire destroyed all but the exterior walls, architect Carlo Mollino was tasked with its reconstruction. His only brief? It must be built within the surviving perimeter.

The building reopened in 1973, new and old connected by a pair of glazed walkways. Red carpet covers every inch of flooring while seemingly floating globes light a labyrinth of stairs under a geometric concrete ceiling which folds like origami. The auditorium is just as impressive, lit by hundreds of glass rods. It is here the theatre truly comes alive, matching its design with rich performances of opera, musicals and more.

Teatro alla Scala
Milan

Designed by architect Giuseppe Piermarini in 1778 while the city was under Austrian rule, the Teatro alla Scala is considered by many to be the "temple of opera". Scores of history's greatest composers, conductors and singers have passed through its neoclassical arches and performed before its red velvet stalls, from Pavarotti and Toscanini to Maria Callas.

Teatro del Maggio Musicale Fiorentino
Florence

Proving there's room yet for opera in the 21st century is Florence's strikingly modern theatre. Designed by Paolo Desideri and opened in 2011, the monolithic structure plays host to three spaces – one a rooftop auditorium. Despite its futuristic look, its programme offers operatic classics from *Madama Butterfly* to *Rinaldo*.

Books:
Novel approach

Publishing is the country's leading cultural industry: around 75,000 titles are released every year. Together with the sector's powerhouses, a plethora of small publishing firms keep the schedule varied – and the shelves of thousands of independent bookshops stocked.

Bookshops
Well read

Just as many Italians choose to pop to the local butcher, greengrocer and bakery for their weekly shop, it's no different when it comes to cultural matters – they still appreciate the act of visiting, and the personal service provided at a bookshop. In fact, over two thirds of all titles bought in Italy are purchased in physical stores as opposed to online. While large (admittedly high-quality) chains such as Feltrinelli, Mondadori and Giunti Editore command the majority of sales, of all the 3,700 bookshops some 2,400 are independent. Their importance in fostering the love of reading and uniting communities remains unmatched – many editors agree they are the most strategic on-the-ground players in disseminating titles and inspiring the next generation.

From sleek purveyors of coffee-table tomes in Milan to Venice's second-hand shops that hide jumbled piles of yellowed novels, bookshops in Italy are as varied as their locales. A vivacious publishing industry ensures there is plenty of new Italian-language fiction (the nation's favourite genre) constantly hitting the shelves. And with legislation to support independents against the industry's behemoths, a new chapter is on the horizon for these cultural stalwarts.

Italy in print

From medieval bards to daring dramaturgs and postmodern pioneers, Italian literature has a rich, varied history: here are a few picks that take us all the way to modern-day bestsellers.

1.
Divine Comedy (1320)
Dante Alighieri
Dante's three-part narrative poem isn't just a paragon of Italian literature but of language too – helping, as it did, shape the Tuscan tongue. While *Purgatorio* and *Paradiso* deal with theological matters, *Inferno* – with its catalogue of sins – is the juiciest read.

2.
Family Lexicon (1963)
Natalia Ginzburg
By zooming in on the minutiae of family life – its intimacy, little rituals, in-jokes and sayings – Ginzburg traces Italian history from the rise of fascism in the 1920s all the way to post-war.

3.
If On a Winter's Night a Traveller (1979)
Italo Calvino
This postmodernist masterpiece is delightfully self-reflective, drawing the reader onto its pages as a character in its story. As most of brilliant intellectual Calvino's writing, it is also riotously fun.

4.
The Shape of Water (1994)
Andrea Camilleri
Sicilian inspector Montalbano began life as the main character in this gripping crime novel before becoming the protagonist of a 28-instalment-long saga (as well as an internationally beloved TV series with Luca Zingaretti in its title role).

5.
My Brilliant Friend (2011)
Elena Ferrante
This global sensation by the mysterious author is Italy's biggest recent publishing hit: the first of the four so-called 'Neapolitan Novels' introduces us to Lila, Lenù and their turbulent friendship.

Music:
All together now

Italians have a penchant for singing, dancing and throwing a proper party – all to a great, homegrown soundtrack, naturally. Besides heart-wrenching ballads and witty songs written by the county's *cantautori* (singer-songwriters often considered nothing short of poets), much of Italy's music is energetic, loud and irresistible on the dancefloor.

Pop music
For the record

A clamorous cacophony with a kaleidoscopic array of vocals and instrumentals, the modern sound of Italy is, at its heart, an ode to melody. It is a score that ranges from slick crooners such as Adriano Celentano and sultry legends like Mina in the 1960s to the persistent na-na-nah guitar-strumming, disco-infused tunes of Umberto Tozzi and Toto Cutugno of the 1970s and Raffaella Carrà's 1980s synthed-up showstoppers.

The melodic (dare we say melodramatic) tendency that defines Italian pop may have its roots in the country's operatic tradition. Although that instantly recognisable chord progression might just as easily trace back to the folk music of Naples. Groups such as Ricchi e Poveri and ultra-corny duo Al Bano & Romina Power used these refrains to great effect, the lyric "*Un bicchiere di vino con un panino*" (A glass of wine with a sandwich) from the 1982 track "Felicità" summing it up best.

This hyper-Italianised sound alienated foreign audiences, though Tozzi's disco banger "Gloria" (1979) was a huge US success for Laura Branigan in 1982 and Carrà is virtually seen as Spain's (or Argentina's) own.

Italian music still had a wide reach in the 1980s – Sabrina Salerno wowed those in the USSR with her bosom-heavy look and addictively repetitious "Boys". Beyond that, a decidedly more vocal, even nasal, strain filled the air in the 1990s and 2000s, Eros Ramazzotti typifying this best followed by Laura Pausini, who rose to fame in 1993 after her Sanremo success. Tiziano Ferro exploded onto the scene in 2001 with his debut "Perdono", which earned him the title of the modern face of Italian pop.

1

2

3

4

7

8

9

10

1.
La Mia Musica (1981)
Toto Cutugno
A decade after winning the Sanremo Festival in 1980, Cutugno went on to become a Eurovision Song Contest victor.

2.
1 (1976)
Matia Bazar
This Genovese band's debut album launched a decades-long career making catchy hits.

3.
Rita Ed Io (1977)
Rita Pavone
The pop icon made it big abroad before returning to present Italian show *Rita ed io*.

4.
Una Storia Importante (1985)
Eros Ramazzotti
Italy's answer to Phil Collins, the 1990s heart-throb found fame in Latin America too.

5.
Voulez Vous Danser (1983)
Ricchi e Poveri
The upbeat, synth-heavy sound of this Genovese outfit filled dance floors across Italy.

6.
Non Sono una Signora (1982)
Loredana Bertè
Björn Borg's second wife, this raspy-voiced singer is known for her eccentric fashion sense as much as her music.

7.
Maschi e Altri (1987)
Gianna Nannini
The Tuscan is famous for her foot-stomping rock anthems.

8.
Boys (1987)
Sabrina
An infamously raunchy music video filmed at a Venetian beach club followed this smash-hit.

9.
Le Più Belle Canzoni (1991)
Al Bano & Romina Power
This album charts decades of heartfelt duets by the former husband and wife duo.

10.
Clown (1982)
Cristiano Malgioglio
As well as releasing his own music, Malgioglio wrote for some of the 1980s' biggest names.

11.
Dolce Far Niente (1984)
Raffaella Carrà
A trained dancer, Carrà made music videos with choreographer husband Sergio Japino.

12.
Erozero (1979)
Renato Zero
Despite his glam-rock look, Zero was known for his take on the sentimental pop ballad.

5

6

11

12

Sanremo Music Festival
This all-singing all-dancing festival started in 1951 as a morale boosting cultural exercise and revival of the once-fashionable Ligurian resort of Sanremo in an Italy still in the shadows of war. Held in February, the Sanremo Music Festival quickly became – and has remained – the way Italians set the musical score for the year ahead by way of hosting musicians to perform yet-to-be released songs.

The festival has frequently launched the careers of its contestants, such as Andrea Bocelli, Giorgia Todrani, Laura Pausini and Eros Ramazzotti. More than that, Sanremo annually draws support and criticism in equal measure – gaffes on the part of hosts and artists or, more recently, political spats have become a feature. Still, its greatest claim to fame is that it reportedly inspired the format for the Eurovision Song Contest, with Sanremo Music Festival now used to determine Italy's entry each year.

Despite the drama, one thing is certain: for five nights every winter, all eyes (and ears) are on Sanremo's Teatro Ariston, where the sound of the nation is decided upon.

Beach clubs
Boogie wonderland

Italians enjoy a night on the tiles year-round but it's in the summer that nightclubs come alive. With a story or two to tell, these seaside *discoteche* are the best spot to watch the sun rise.

La Capannina di Franceschi, Forte dei Marmi
Opened in 1929, this club in Tuscany's Forte dei Marmi claims to be the world's oldest disco. When its first owner Achille Franceschi acquired it, the Capannina was nothing more than a hut on the beach with a bar, gramophone and a few tables. By the 1930s it had become a trendy spot for aristocrats and intellectuals to sip Negronis while later on, cinema stars, industrialists and royals began to frequent the place. Over the years, musicians by the likes of Édith Piaf, Ray Charles, Gino Paoli and Patty Pravo have played here. Owned by Gherardo and Carla Guidi since 1977, the Capannina's dance floor still fills at night to the sound of disco.

Covo di Nord Est, Santa Margherita Ligure
Perched on a cliff between Liguria's Portofino and Santa Margherita, this club is worth a visit for its location alone. Intended as a residence for a local baron's lover, construction began in 1898 but stopped upon the heartbroken nobleman's tragic death. It opened its doors in 1934 as a club, attracting the rich (who'd moor directly onto its pontoon) through to its 1970s heyday. An outdoor dance floor juts out on the panoramic terrace while five bars and four restaurants hide within and a private *bagni* resides below.

Raya, Panarea
Car-free Panarea is the smallest of Sicily's Aeolian Islands and most arrive by boat. Though the isle's atmosphere may be blissfully unspoilt (albeit upscale), Hotel Raya's nightclub ensures raucous fun can be enjoyed too. Open from late July to the end of August, the club has welcomed internationally renowned DJs and hosts the annual electronic festival Raya Summer Fest.

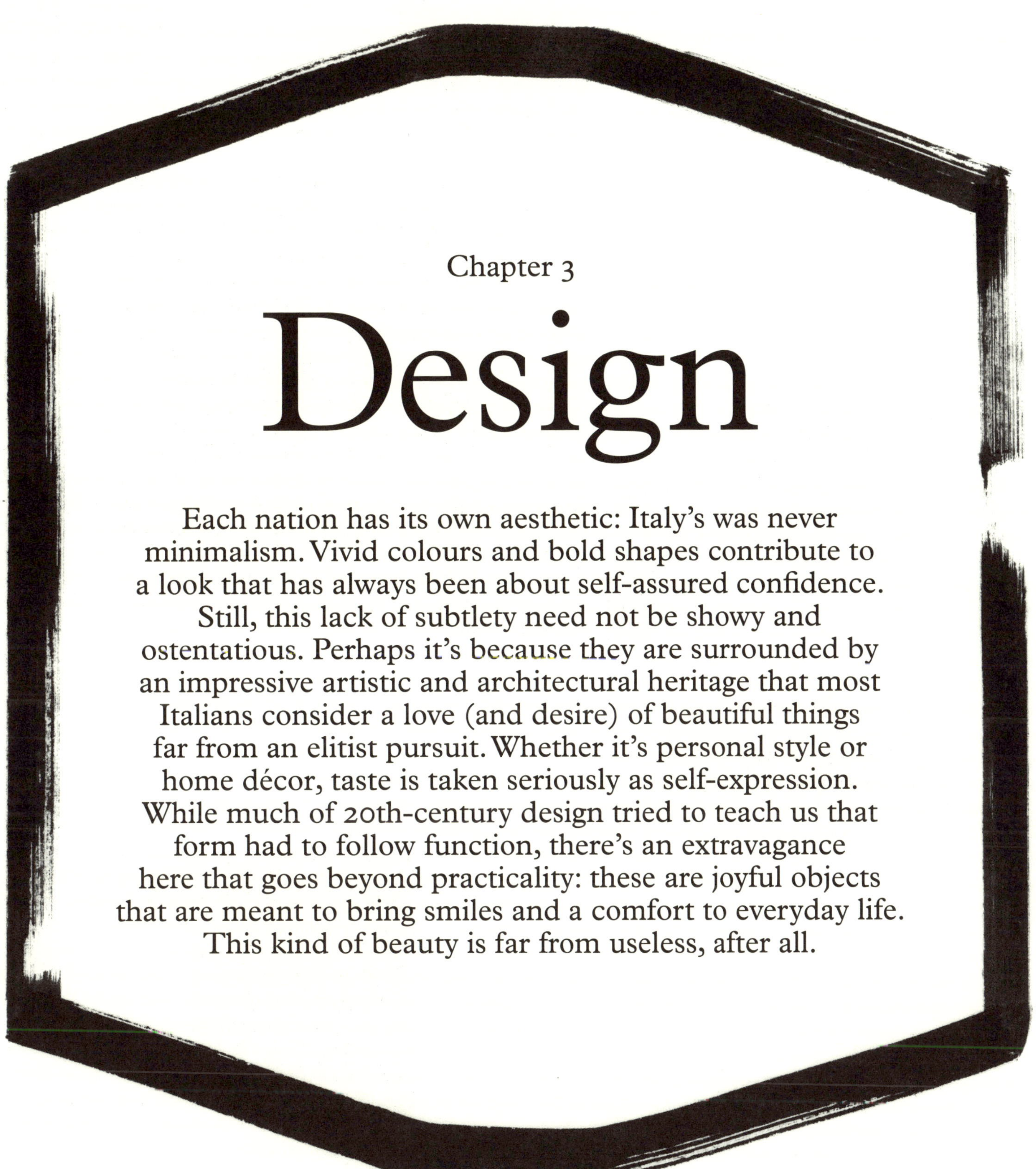

Chapter 3

Design

Each nation has its own aesthetic: Italy's was never minimalism. Vivid colours and bold shapes contribute to a look that has always been about self-assured confidence. Still, this lack of subtlety need not be showy and ostentatious. Perhaps it's because they are surrounded by an impressive artistic and architectural heritage that most Italians consider a love (and desire) of beautiful things far from an elitist pursuit. Whether it's personal style or home décor, taste is taken seriously as self-expression. While much of 20th-century design tried to teach us that form had to follow function, there's an extravagance here that goes beyond practicality: these are joyful objects that are meant to bring smiles and a comfort to everyday life. This kind of beauty is far from useless, after all.

Interiors: *Design heroes*

Italians have turned their colourful, playful aesthetic sense into a huge business. From soft armchairs to brilliant lamps, meet the sector's brightest stars.

Furniture
Sitting pretty

Italy's genesis as the crucible of contemporary furniture design was down to a well-aligned set of factors. Modernist lines emerged early on: rationalist architects such as Giuseppe Terragni were thinking up sleek items to furnish their built creations back in the 1930s. But it was the immediate postwar period – that so pressingly called for new houses, new means of filling them and a new way of living – that propelled Italy to furniture greatness. The area close to Milan became, and still is, the industry's epicentre. The style, mood and quantity of architects in the Lombard capital was one reason for its success. From Gio Ponti to Osvaldo Borsani, they not only dabbled in the design of chairs and tables but made them the utmost expression of their skills as maestros.

Today, giants such as B&B Italia, Porada, Cassina, Poliform, Flexform, Molteni&C and Rimadesio are setting the global standard with collaborations with world-renowned designers – and carrying out intensive R&D activity with unrivalled workshops and purpose-built facilities. Danish furniture may have minimalism and German designs functionality but it's not until you sink into a huge, soft Italian sofa that you understand homes also need to be bold, welcoming and warm.

Lighting

Like so much that is designed and made in Italy, lighting has its own bright history. It's hard to trace the origins of this Italian specialism, although the centuries-old tradition for blown glass lamps and chandeliers made in Murano shines a suitably opulent light on the subject.

The surrounding Veneto area is still considered the country's illumination hub with outfits such as Foscarini and Axolight making decidedly hi-tech, LED renditions of their Venetian forbears. In classic Italian fashion, however, the industry is far from being the concern of just one single region.

In Milan, many showrooms by the country's most illustrious producers – including Flos, FontanaArte and Nemo – are clustered along Corso Monforte in the Durini area. Just outside the Lombard city, the Artemide factory makes some of the field's most recognisable lamps, including the likes of the ever-popular Tolomeo series designed by Michele De Lucchi and Giancarlo Fassina.

The glow also spreads further south: iGuzzini, based in the Marche region, is the largest indoor and outdoor illumination specialist in the whole nation.

Clockwise from far left: an armchair is crafted at the Molteni&C factory; Six Gallery in Milan; Cassina's Milan showroom; an eye-catching pendant at Milan's Nilufar Depot; a Tulip table by Eero Saarinen is made at Knoll's marble factory; the UP50 Lounge chair by B&B Italia; Gio Ponti's D.655.1 sideboard at Molteni&C

Kitchens

The "fitted kitchen" with its neat, flush arrangement of surfaces sandwiched between handy cabinets above and below is largely an Italian creation. Given the country's artisanal credentials, it is little surprise that brands such as Arclinea, Snaidero and Boffi started applying their talents to creating fine furniture for the kitchen.

Materials:
Make it better

Hardly any phrase elicits more pride across the nation than "Made in Italy". All citizens grow up with a deep-seated knowledge of the value and intrinsic quality the expression signifies. Many of the country's biggest industries and exports are rooted in time-honoured crafts that began as artisanal pursuits – and, in their updated formats, many of those traditions survive today.

Glass
Clear cut

The ancient art of glassblowing is synonymous with Murano. This small island in the Venetian lagoon has been home to glassblowers since 1291, when the government of Venice relocated them in order to protect the secrets of their techniques (and also the city from their fierce furnaces).

Those practices are no longer quite so closely guarded, yet nowhere else has managed to recreate the dexterity of Murano's glassmakers, most of whom descend from generations in the craft and employ the same methods used for centuries. Only the designs are new – and have been renewed over the years – as the craftspeople at Murano's top makers, such as Salviati and Venini, have attracted some of Italy's most respected designers.

Production here will never be industrial, as the three-man dance that shapes each item can only proceed at an artisan's pace. Due to the physicality and the customs of the production process, the craftspeople remain largely male, though a new era of external collaborations is increasingly bringing female input into the furnaces. As glass finds a new audience, the old techniques continue to adapt to new styles – but Murano remains unrivalled.

Ceramics
Bowled over

For centuries, Italian artisans have excelled at crafting vivid earthenware and certain destinations such as Faenza in Emilia-Romagna and Sicily's Caltagirone have become famed for their ceramic offerings.

In Tuscany, two prominent examples have persisted over time. One is family-run Bitossi: in 1921, the brand established and nurtured a collaboration with a number of creatives, including architect, designer and general polymath Ettore Sottsass, who conceived an imaginative collection of vases and bowls. But perhaps best known is its cerulean-hued series, Rimini Blu, designed by Aldo Londi.

The other is Richard Ginori, founded in 1735, which has enjoyed a long and glorious history thanks to its high-end tableware. Among the firm's most prolific periods was the decade-long tenure of architect Gio Ponti as artistic director, who deftly modernised the traditional manufacturer with the help of in-house artisans.

Today, as companies such as tile-maker Mutina continue to collect contemporary designers, the country's prowess in all things ceramic remains undisputed – especially given the main architectural ceramics fair, Cersaie, takes place in Bologna every year.

Textiles
Material world

Italy's dominance in the world of high fashion begins with its textiles. In the domain of luxury apparel, the country supplies an estimated 90 per cent of all fabrics; of the world's cloth, Italy provides 7 per cent.

Widely considered the finest quality in the world, Italian textiles hail from specialised areas around the nation that trace their manufacturing roots back centuries: when Silk Road knowledge transformed the lakeside town of Como into a mulberry tree-filled, silk-making powerhouse, or when the shepherds' fields of Biella began weaving the finest wool for the Duke of Savoy.

The most renowned textile manufacturers today – the silk factories of Mantero, Ratti and Mosconi in Como; the wool weavers of Loro Piana, Zegna and Vitale Barberis Canonico in Biella; Bonotto with its art-influenced fabrics in Vicenza – descend from the storied roots of such districts. Their success is underscored by one of Italy's best manufacturing qualities: the ability to fuse artisan tradition and industrial capabilities with innovation and creativity.

Design icons:
Creative flair

There isn't too much subtlety in the products that define Italian design history: curvaceous, eye-popping and riotously fun, these are objects that bring a smile to the everyday. Many still feature in their unchanged vintage forms today.

Illy espresso cup
Co-founder of Memphis Milano, the flamboyant postmodern design movement, Matteo Thun created these heat-retaining cups in 1992 – they can hold piping-hot espresso to be consumed in one gulp.

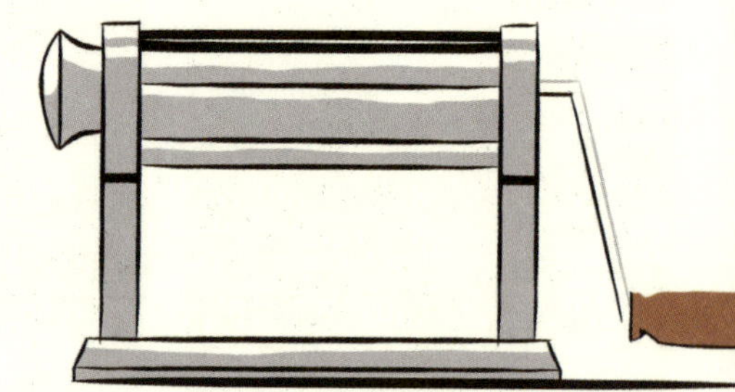

Imperia pasta machine
Imperia was established as a small metalworking business in 1932 but expanded rapidly as their durable and easy-to-use pasta machines gained popularity, particularly among Italian immigrants in the USA who wanted to recreate the taste of home.

Bialetti moka pot
When engineer Alfonso Bialetti noticed a gap in the market for an espresso-making appliance for use in the home, he set about developing this octagonal stove-top coffee pot. The first model was produced in 1933 and today bears his moustachioed caricature.

Classic Fiat 500
First produced in 1957, the Fiat 500 was designed by Dante Giacosa as a cheap-and-cheerful pint-sized vehicle with the agility needed to navigate narrow city streets.

Zenith stapler
Balma, Capoduri & Co has been making Zenith staplers since 1948. Its sturdy design (each comes with a lifetime guarantee) is the work of inventor Aldo Balma.

Eclisse lamp
Designed in 1965, Vico Magistretti's compact metal lamp is inspired by the lunar eclipse. It has a fixed outer shell while its inner shade can be rotated to diffuse the bulb's intensity.

Arco lamp
Pier Giacomo and Achille Castiglioni's ubiquitous lamp was first made by lighting brand Flos in 1962. It has a Carrara marble base and adjustable stainless-steel stem.

Valentine typewriter
Ettore Sottsass's 1969 model (co-designed with Perry King) for Olivetti was manufactured as a dinky Italian competitor to the inexpensive Japanese designs that were flooding the market. To make it cheaper, Sottsass did away with lower case letters and the bell that marked the end of each line.

699 Superleggera chair
Gio Ponti's Leggera chair was first made by Cassina in 1952 and refined to produce the Superleggera in 1957, famously tested when Ponti dropped it from a fourth-floor window.

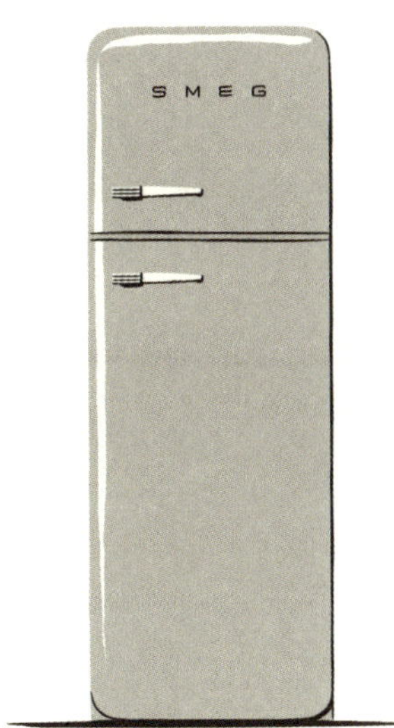

Smeg fridge
Kitchen appliance-maker Smeg produced its retro-style Fab28 fridge in 1997. Designed by founder Vittorio Bertazzoni, it comes in a series with matching toasters, kettles and more.

Il conico kettle
Architect Aldo Rossi (the first Italian to be awarded the Pritzker Prize) transposed the conical motif on many of his buildings to form the Piedmontese homeware brand Alessi's stainless-steel kettle in 1986.

Vespa Piaggio
At the end of the Second World War, aeronautical engineer Corradino D'Ascanio was asked to design an easily ridden vehicle that could be mass-produced; the Vespa ("wasp") swarmed Italian cities from 1946.

Pasta cutter
A staple in Italian homes, this nifty bit of kitchen kit is rolled across sheets of fresh pasta to add scalloped edges to ravioli. The wheels are interchangeable to allow the user to adjust the depth of the cuts.

Spaghetti lounger
Fiam founder Francesco Favagrossa launched his outdoor furniture firm in 1975. Made from PVC strips woven around an aluminium frame, this lounger is bouncy and comfortable.

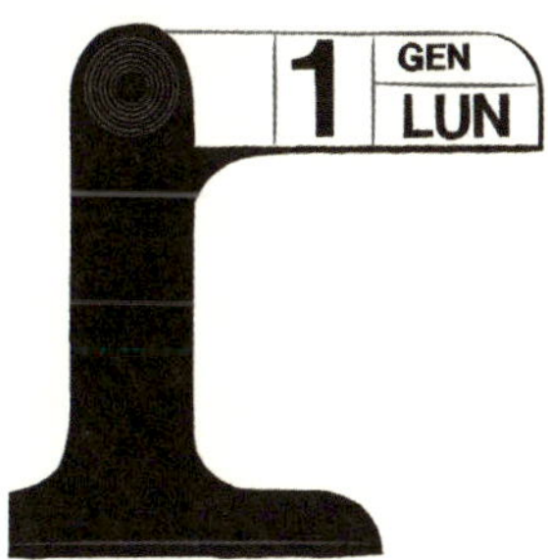

Timor calendar
A prominent name in 20th-century Italian design, Enzo Mari was known for the playfulness of his creations. His desk calendar for Danese Milano in 1967 uses flippable PVC cards.

Graphic design: *Making a brand*

Italian graphic design hasn't always enjoyed the attention it deserves. Many of Italy's world-leading companies have called on the country's designers to conceive branding to match their character.

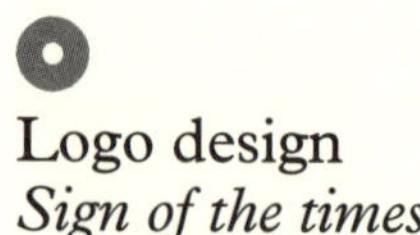

Logo design
Sign of the times

Defining the quintessential Italian logo is no mean feat. In a country with such a varied visual and regional history it is hard to talk about nation-based aesthetic principles. There is, however, a boldness and brand coherence that might be recognised as Italian.

There are two main reasons for this, says Gabriele Oropallo, a lecturer in visual cultures and design history: "Italy was in the second wave of countries to industrialise but it already had a strong avant garde design tradition." Booming companies had the luxury of some of the world's top typographers and graphic designers on their doorstep. People such as Max Huber, Bob Noorda and Massimo Vignelli spent the 1950s and 1960s creating logos and typesets that still dominate today.

This trendsetting visual language was also based on tradition; the importance of the sign or manifesto is timeless in Italy. Starting with the Roman alphabet to the battles between city states, the Italians have always had a flair for the act of demonstration. From flashing neon to a pasticceria's packaging, brazen typesets and archetypical logos still adorn modern Italy.

1.
Alitalia
Walter Landor won the 1969 global competition to design the airline's logo using the colours of the Italian flag and a bold rounded lettering. The tail-shaped "A" is a device that applies easily to company material from boarding passes to napkins.

2.
Prada
As an official supplier of the House of Savoy, Prada was allowed to feature the royal family's heraldry in its emblem. Miuccia Prada stripped this back when she took over in the 1970s, although the logo does still occasionally appear in its original form.

3.
Mondadori
Bob Noorda is the man behind many of Italy's best-known marks. His 1969 work for publisher Mondadori features the founder Arnoldo Mondadori's first initials and uses a chunky, geometric typeface with an exaggerated serif.

4.
Salvatore Ferragamo
The Florentine shoemaker's logo has had various iterations since its conception in 1927 but to honour Salvatore Ferragamo's death in 1960 the brand reverted to his signature. It was updated in 1982 to make it appear thicker and more legible.

5.
Nutella
When Ferrero launched its hazelnut chocolate spread in 1964, Gian Rossetti and Carmelo Cremonesi of Milan's Studio Stile were called in to create the logo. The result was a simple Helvetica Medium typeset of the brand name that has become instantly recognisable.

6.
Coop
The sign of Italy's largest supermarket chain is the work of Milanese designer Albe Steiner. To represent its status as a cooperative and suggest unity, he used a looping style that brings together four adjacent circles.

1 Alitalia

2 PRADA

3 GRUPPO MONDADORI

4 Salvatore Ferragamo

5 nutella®

6

Advertising
Pitch perfect

Graphic design played a fundamental role in the process of establishing the economic and entrepreneurial success of "Made in Italy" brands. It was a vital representation of the quality of products and of their modern, exciting, almost revolutionary nature. Italian-made items have long been associated with originality, elegance and innate style: graphic design shaped the symbolic set of visual references through which consumers got to know these objects. Before owning a chair, an armchair, a sofa or a kitchen appliance, perspective buyers got to know their names, their shapes and their innovative features from posters, adverts and catalogues. These works have left their mark in the history of communications.

Clockwise from top: Giovanni Pintori for Olivetti (1962); Giovanni Pintori for Underwood (1961); Enrico Ciuti for Triennale di Milano (1940); Bob Noorda for Pirelli (1957); Massimo Vignelli for Pirelli (1963); Enrico Ciuti for Tecno (1956)

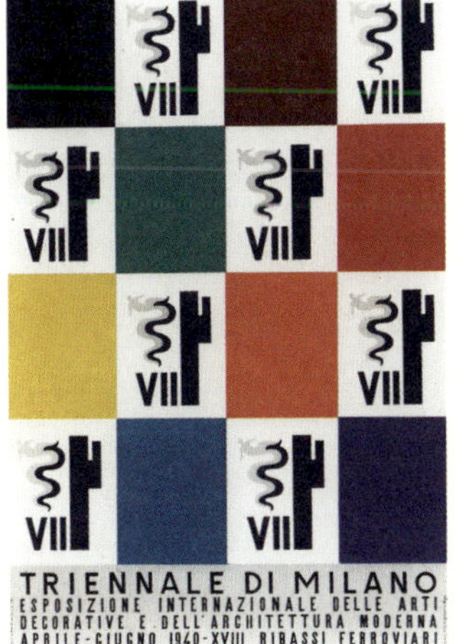

Five graphic designers

1.
Giulio Confalonieri
Leafing through 1960s design and architecture magazines, Confalonieri's name – paired with that of his business partner Ilio Negri – appears notably often. Together, they formed Studio Industria: the duo combined different visual styles to striking effect, shaping the identity of companies like Boffi in the process.

2.
Michele Provinciali
Thinking about objects outside their normal context and letting them speak their own language was Provinciali's hallmark trait. This method – an ability to turn forms into symbols – was his strategy in building business for big brands such as Kartell.

3.
Enrico Ciuti
Ciuti was a forerunner in the art of creating a virtuous relationship between architects and graphic designers. He worked with the likes of Marcello Nizzoli and Gio Ponti.

4.
Bob Noorda
Together with Italian Massimo Vignelli (and other American partners), Dutch-born designer Bob Noorda founded agency Unimark International in 1965 across Italy and the US. Its highly organised approach was successful in landing jobs with huge multinationals.

5.
Giovanni Pintori
Working at typewriter-maker Olivetti for decades (finally becoming its art director in 1950) meant that Sardinian-born Pintori had an unmatched influence in defining the feel of this icon of Italian product design.

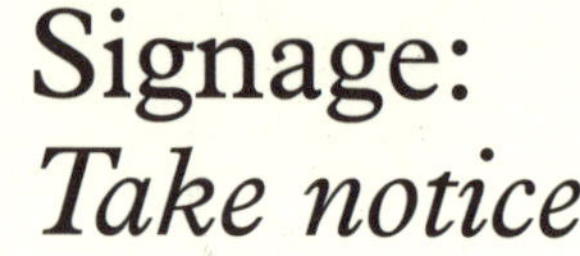

Signage:
Take notice

Italy's retail landscape is still blessed with a multitude of independent shops: each is unique and bears its own signage. From bold typography to free-flowing, hand-painted letterforms, these signs are an integral part of a city's identity.

DA GIGGETTO
SPECIALITÀ ROMANE

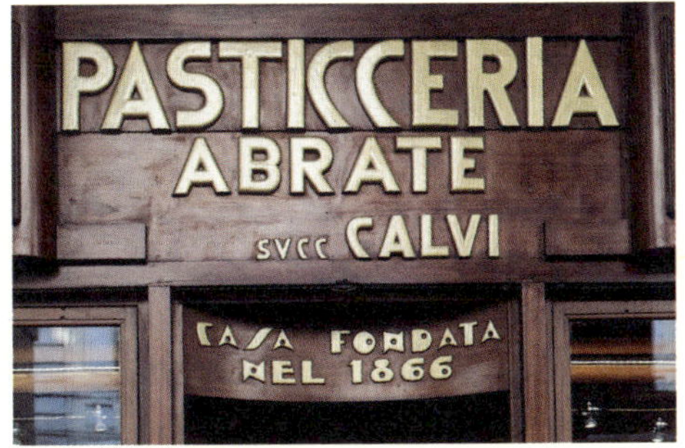
PASTICCERIA
ABRATE
SVCC CALVI
CASA FONDATA
NEL 1866

Lavanderia
Carla

TABACCHI
Bonzano

PARRUCCHIERE

Baratti & Milano

G.NNI VALLONE
CUOIAMI

ELETTRICITA'

FINOLLO

Stagno

Nuovo
Nazionale

ELVETICO

AUTORIPARAZIONI
MECCANICA

BANCO DI SICILIA

Morutto
STRUMENTI MUSICALI
MORUTTO
MUSICA

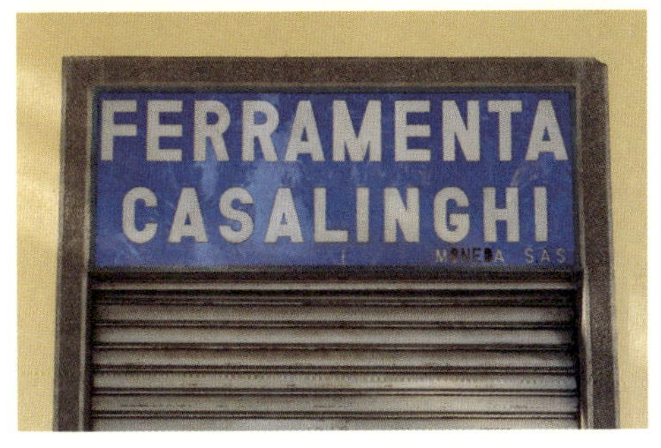
FERRAMENTA
CASALINGHI

Specchi
Cornici

FORMAGGI

Fashion week:
Strike a pose

New York Fashion Week has the commercial brands; London the provocateurs; Paris the historic maisons. And Milan? Milan has the family-run powerhouses. What the city's fashion week schedule lacks in young names it makes up for with its cadre of titans who rose up in the 1980s and have been setting the global fashion agenda ever since.

Four times a year – twice for men and twice for women – editors, buyers and stylists gather to see creations from Miuccia Prada, Donatella Versace, Giorgio Armani and Silvia Venturini Fendi (and also from brands including Missoni and Salvatore Ferragamo). These designers' surnames *are* their brand names – a pretty rare thing in today's luxury industry. The very streets of the city become one long catwalk: this is *sprezzatura* (stylish insouciance) at its very best.

But Italian fashion has a second ace up its perfectly tailored sleeve: menswear buyers also head to Florence for Pitti Uomo, the world's leading men's fashion tradeshow. In the sprawling grounds, visitors get a feel for upcoming trends where they can touch fabrics and see garments up close – and it's also a chance to brazenly show off impeccable suits and old-school ties and lapels.

Fashion brands:
Wardrobe wonders

Away from the glitz of the runway, a host of smaller independent brands are making the most of the nation's vast array of textiles and materials with an approach that prizes tactility and longevity. These are designs that last beyond just one season.

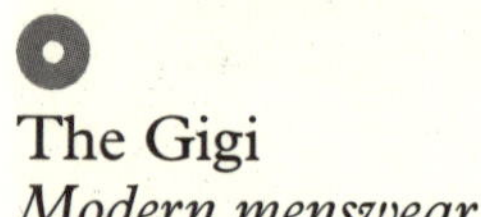

The Gigi
Modern menswear

Pierluigi Boglioli has tailoring in his blood. Raised by clothier parents, he joined the family business Boglioli in the 1990s and helped it develop a fresh and more contemporary look that caught the eye of discerning sartorialists around the world. Keen for a new challenge, he left the company in 2013 to found his own brand alongside his brother Mario.

"In a small company you can be braver," says Pierluigi. "The Gigi is young, flexible and future-facing but it's led by people with more than 40 years of experience in the fashion industry."

The result is an informal take on fine Italian tailoring from slouchy double-breasted blazers and slim-fitting wool trousers to luxurious knitwear. The brand's finishing touch comes in the form of Pierluigi's telling motto, which is stitched into each of his designs: "Don't look back".

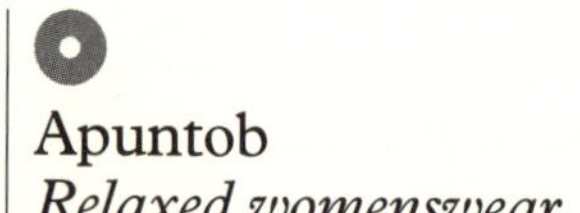

Apuntob
Relaxed womenswear

Designer Barbara Garofalo founded her women's clothing brand in 2006, naming it Apuntob (A dot B) after her grandmother, Angela Brunozzi, an early-1900s hat designer. Garofalo describes her pieces as "uncomplicated, everyday fashion but made really well". Each collection starts with a vision of colour, from Rothko one season to a blue-toned photo of a beach bungalow the next, and bespoke fabrics that she develops with Italian and Japanese textile manufacturers. "I refuse to use the same fabrics that everyone else is using," she says.

Her designs – breezy linen trousers, shift dresses and relaxed blazers – "are quiet enough that a woman is never lost in them," she continues. "They look different on everyone because they let a woman's character show through. They are a thinking-woman's clothes."

Barena Venezia
Contemporary casual

Barena's tale is firmly rooted in Veneto. It was started in 1961 by Sandro Zara who named his venture after Venice's famed lagoons (the *barena* is where the water is at its shallowest). In 1993, he teamed up with Massimo Pigozzo, a fellow Veneto native who had worked as a designer in Milan, to create Barena's inaugural collection. In the years since, the label has steadily worked its way into the world's most discerning retailers – including a collaboration with MONOCLE – and the brand now credits a womenswear range, designed by Zara's daughter Francesca (*pictured*), to its name.

Pigozzo and Zara's lines are conceived separately, though they share a spirit of easy elegance, from Pigozzo's relaxed blazers or Zara's tailored shirt-dresses and loose-fitting trousers. "You don't need to be wild or complicated to be cool," says Zara. "We design what we like to wear."

Massimo Alba
Soft tailoring

Massimo Alba has designed clothes since the 1980s but it wasn't until 2006 that his eponymous brand was born and his supremely soft knitwear began to garner a following. It has since increased its offering to include unstructured jackets, slim trousers and shirts in luxurious cottons and linens.

When it came to opening a shop in his hometown of Milan, Alba chose a site close to the Orto Botanico and papered the walls with pages from gardening journals. "I love nature. All the colours I use are drawn from the natural world." Comfort and tactility are also key with items washed and dyed to remove the rigid feel of unworn clothes. "Everything we make is soft," he says. "We want our clothes to offer emotional comfort too."

Chapter 4

Architecture

Few activities are as effective as taking a stroll around the centre of Rome to realise that most Italian cities are an accumulation of layers of history. Styles from different eras coexist happily in a captivating collage. Not all places display their ancient heritage in the same obvious way as the capital, but it's easy to forget how much of our built environment (in Italy and beyond) was shaped by the Romans. They were responsible for many of the fundamental building blocks of urbanism that we have grown accustomed to: from roads and aqueducts to arches, domes and even concrete, they were the original town planners. Still, many cities owe their visual identities to the "patron" architects who shaped their appearances: from Filippo Juvarra's baroque imprint on Turin to Carlo Scarpa's rethinking of Venice's relationship with water and Gio Ponti's modern Milanese visions, these masters have left their own mark on these crowded urban landscapes.

Ten buildings:
Site seeing

Italy's long and august history means that buildings of numerous styles and periods often coexist in the same city. Not just mementos, these structures have provided recurring inspiration for new projects through the decades.

1.
Fiat Lingotto factory (1923)
Turin

Designed by naval architect and engineer Giacomo Mattè-Trucco, Fiat's Lingotto factory is the architectural embodiment of the production line. Raw materials entered from the ground floor and, as the cars began to take shape, they climbed an internal ramp that snaked its way through the five storeys – each performing a different function. At the top, a fully formed vehicle would emerge onto the 1km-long test track on the roof.

When it opened it was the largest (and arguably most impressive, as Le Corbusier once attested) car factory in the world. Production stopped in 1982, but not before it had developed 80 Fiat models and established Turin – and Italy – as a hub of innovation. In 1989, the complex was reimagined by Renzo Piano with an exhibition centre, two hotels, retail space and more.

2.

Torre Velasca (1958)

Milan

There are certain buildings that cause you to stop in your tracks. The imposing Torre Velasca – which rises from its low-lying Milanese neighbourhood like a mutation between an air-traffic control building and a medieval watchtower – compels you to crane your neck for a better view of its outline.

A product of Milan's postwar industrial boom years and built on an area that had been flattened by bomb damage, the 106-metre reinforced concrete structure was the design of BBPR studio, founded by partners including Ernesto Nathan Rogers (cousin of architect Richard Rogers).

The building remains mixed-use today with the lower levels dedicated to shops and office space while the increased floorplan of the upper storeys houses some of the city's most exclusive apartments.

3. The Pantheon (1st century BC) *Rome*

The ancient Romans knew a thing or two about construction. The Pantheon – a pagan temple dedicated to all the gods past, present and future – can still lay claim to the largest unreinforced concrete dome in the world, nearly 2,000 years after it was built. Experts attribute its longevity to the specific blend of limestone and volcanic ash used in the mortar.

The current structure is the result of remodelling work by Emperor Hadrian (he of wall fame) between 120AD and 128AD, after the original building was destroyed by a fire. In 609AD it became the first Roman temple to be consecrated as a Christian church and the building has been in continuous use throughout its history. It has no windows – the only light source is the oculus in the dome.

4. San Giorgio Maggiore (1610)

Venice

How to choose just one historic church from Italy's embarrassment of Renaissance riches and baroque beauties? Truth be told, we could have picked almost any, but Andrea Palladio's San Giorgio Maggiore in Venice is proof of Italy's influence on international design.

Palladio was a 16th-century starchitect who took elements of ancient Greek and Roman design and combined them with the humanist ideals of the Renaissance, creating a style based on symmetry that would influence later generations of architects and dominate Western aesthetics for centuries.

The church's classical white exterior with its pair of stacked pediments took decades to construct (Palladio never saw it completed in his lifetime) and the bright interior is hung with works by Tintoretto.

5.
Concattedrale Gran Madre di Dio (1970)
Taranto

This geometric cathedral in the southern port-city of Taranto – which from a distance looks like it could be made of matchsticks – is the work of Gio Ponti, the architect and designer perhaps best known for the 699 Superleggera chair (*see page 159*) and Milan's Pirelli Tower. The filigree-style structure was inspired by paper cut-outs and has been likened to a ship – instead of a dome or spire, Ponti chose an immense central tower which looms behind the façade like a hoisted sail.

The interiors are equally captivating with a sea-green colour palette continuing the maritime feel across everything from the tiled floors to the bronze doors. There are even two concrete columns topped by crosses that have been subtly stylised as anchors – truly putting the naval into nave.

Gio Ponti
Founder of *Domus* magazine, the revered architect designed just about everything – over six decades he drew up plans for cars, coffee machines and countless buildings.

6.
Palazzo della Civiltà Italiana (1942)
Rome

There's more to Rome's architectural vernacular than gilded domes and ionic columns, as this bombastic travertine cube (commissioned by none other than Benito Mussolini) attests. The Palazzo della Civiltà Italiana – sometimes referred to as the *Colosseo Quadrato* (Square Colosseum) – is part of a district called EUR on the outskirts of the capital, which was originally designed to host the cancelled 1942 World's Fair.

Perhaps the clearest example of the fascist regime's architecture and urban planning programme, it is packed with overt devices to glorify ancient Rome and Italian history and culture. In 2015 the building became home to the HQ of luxury fashion brand Fendi – not without a dose of controversy.

7. Oberholz Mountain Hut (2016)

South Tyrol

The Dolomites are home to many of Italy's most groundbreaking contemporary buildings. This mountain-hut project which opened in 2016 is a collaboration between South Tyrol native Peter Pichler and Slovak-born, Bolzano-based Pavol Mikolajcak. It features a triumvirate of handsome gable-roofed, cantilevered structures which fan out to face the surrounding peaks.

The glass-fronted façades are striking but it's the interior – a sort of modernist take on the traditional chalet – that is perhaps the building's most spellbinding feature. The walls and ceilings are dominated by a giant wooden ribcage which opens out into a space that is a play on the South Tyrolean *Stube* – a wood-panelled parlour found in local farmhouses, restaurants and hotels.

8. Casa Malaparte (1938) *Capri*

Capri might be best known as a place to top up the tan and sip a sundowner but those willing to venture away from the lounger will discover that it's also home to one of Italy's most fascinating residences. The big caveat here is that Casa Malaparte (named after the journalist and intellectual who commissioned Adalberto Libera to design the house but, ultimately, discarded said plans in favour of his own) remains a private property, so you're going to have to find a clever vantage point.

Located on a remote nugget of coastline, the villa – essentially a long, red rectangle tipped with a cinematic staircase and topped with a vast sun terrace – is considered one of Italy's finest examples of Rationalist architecture and has starred in more than its fair share of perfume ads.

9.

Brion cemetery (1978)
San Vito d'Altivole

This concrete tomb was built as an extension to the municipal cemetry of the town of San Vito d'Altivole in Veneto. Commissioned by Onorina Brion Tomasin in memory of her husband Giuseppe, founder of the Brionvega electronics company, the structure – which was one of Carlo Scarpa's last major works – features interconnected spaces including a chapel, water pavilion and burial site set among gardens dotted with Italian cypress trees.

The complex is loaded with symbolism – circles and water are thought to represent eternity and reflection – while Scarpa's fascination with Japan is evident in the geometric panels reminiscent of shoji screens. Upon his death in 1978, Scarpa was buried (standing upright) in the plot, according to the detailed instructions in his will.

10.
Bosco Verticale (2014)
Milan

The arrival of Milan's "vertical forest", a pair of towers designed by Studio Boeri, marked something of a watershed moment for the city – an eye-catching contemporary structure that cemented the cachet of the Isola neighbourhood. Constructed between 2007 and 2014, the towers feature some 900 trees, shrubs and other flora which spill over the balconies and out of the rooftop spaces.

Bringing some much needed greenery to Milan – it is equivalent to 20,000 sq m of standard forest – the project also acts as a neat filtering system for the city's smog, absorbing CO_2 and dust particles. It has won the approval of both the jury of the International Highrise Award in 2014 and the local insect population, and has inspired plenty of copycats abroad.

Carlo Scarpa
Born in Venice in 1906, Scarpa shaped the modern aesthetic of his city like no other – quite an achievement considering he never formalised his architecture studies.

Communities:
Three case studies

Stark differences in the country's topography mean there is no single architectural vernacular in Italy. However, there is one theme that tends to be present from north to south: community. From Mitteleuropean-influenced mountain residences to stone-built Mediterranean stomping grounds, we tour the peninsula and its islands to reveal some models for living.

Mountain getaway
Borca di Cadore, Belluno

In the early 1950s businessman Enrico Mattei had a utopian vision: to build a modernist mountain retreat where workers and their families could get close to nature. As head of Italy's state oil firm, Eni, Mattei wanted to offer employees the chance of an alpine holiday, something beyond their reach as such tourism was still the domain of the well-to-do.

In 1954 Mattei singled out a hillside above the town of Borca di Cadore with postcard-perfect views of Mount Pelmo. He enlisted the help of architect Edoardo Gellner to design Corte di Cadore, a complex of two-bedroomed cottages, two hotels, a holiday retreat for 600 children and a church.

Over time, it drew fewer Eni vacationers and fell into neglect but its fortunes were turned around in 2001 when Gualtiero Cualbu, head of Sardinian construction firm Minoter, became enamoured with the site. Minoter diligently restored the roofs and interiors and has been selling the lodges to architecture aficionados and those looking for a quiet spot. "It's more a labour of love than a real-estate investment," says manager Giuseppe Cualbu, the owner's son who also holidays in the family's cottage. "It's secluded, has great views and is unlike anything around it."

Beachside resort
Puntaldia, Sardinia

Sun, sand and sustained Italian postwar wealth were brought together to create Puntaldia in the early 1980s. The 700 or so apartments, residences and villas that make up the resort on Sardinia's glitzy northeast coast sit amid rolling hills, which fold down to a sparkling marina and beach.

Developer Peppino Fumagalli called on Milanese architect Gianni Gamondi to design Puntaldia and gave him a brief to accentuate the locale's natural beauty while referencing the vernacular of Sardinian homes. Gamondi built the complex from materials typical of the island: pink rocks from the fields and white granite from caves. All of the tiles on the roofs were recovered from dilapidated buildings on the island.

The approach attracted a tasteful Italian set, largely Milanese and Roman, who snapped up their second homes here at a startling rate. "We bought this house in 1997," says Daniela Scalvenzi from one of the late-1990s villas her family owns (the Missoni family of fashion fame owns another). "I've been coming here since I was eight. It's very easy here, it's so quiet. We're surrounded by nature – you live with the simplicity and beauty of the place and your friends."

Urban development
Villaggio Olimpico, Rome

As you hurtle along Rome's ancient Via Flaminia and veer east there is little to indicate you are approaching something of a modernist urban marvel, tucked just south of the Tiber.

The first clue to the area's past is the concrete dome of Pier Luigi Nervi's Palazzetto dello Sport. It was built to accommodate tournaments during the Olympics, which Rome hosted in 1960. Beyond is one of the world's first purpose-built athletes' villages, the Villaggio Olimpico. Overseen by two of Italy's most renowned architects, Luigi Moretti and Adalberto Libera, it was designed to house 6,500 competitors and provide residences after the games.

Today the infrastructure is well used by those who call it home. "Here I think good architecture makes good residents," says architectural conservationist Simona Salvo. She's one of a growing class of creatives in the area, drawn by the green surroundings and mid-century housing stock. In Salvo's part of the complex you can see straight across the village: aside from a few slender pillars, the occasional lemon tree or parked Fiat Panda, the view is unimpaired. "We can see our children playing," says Salvo. "We have a wonderful balance of privacy and comfort."

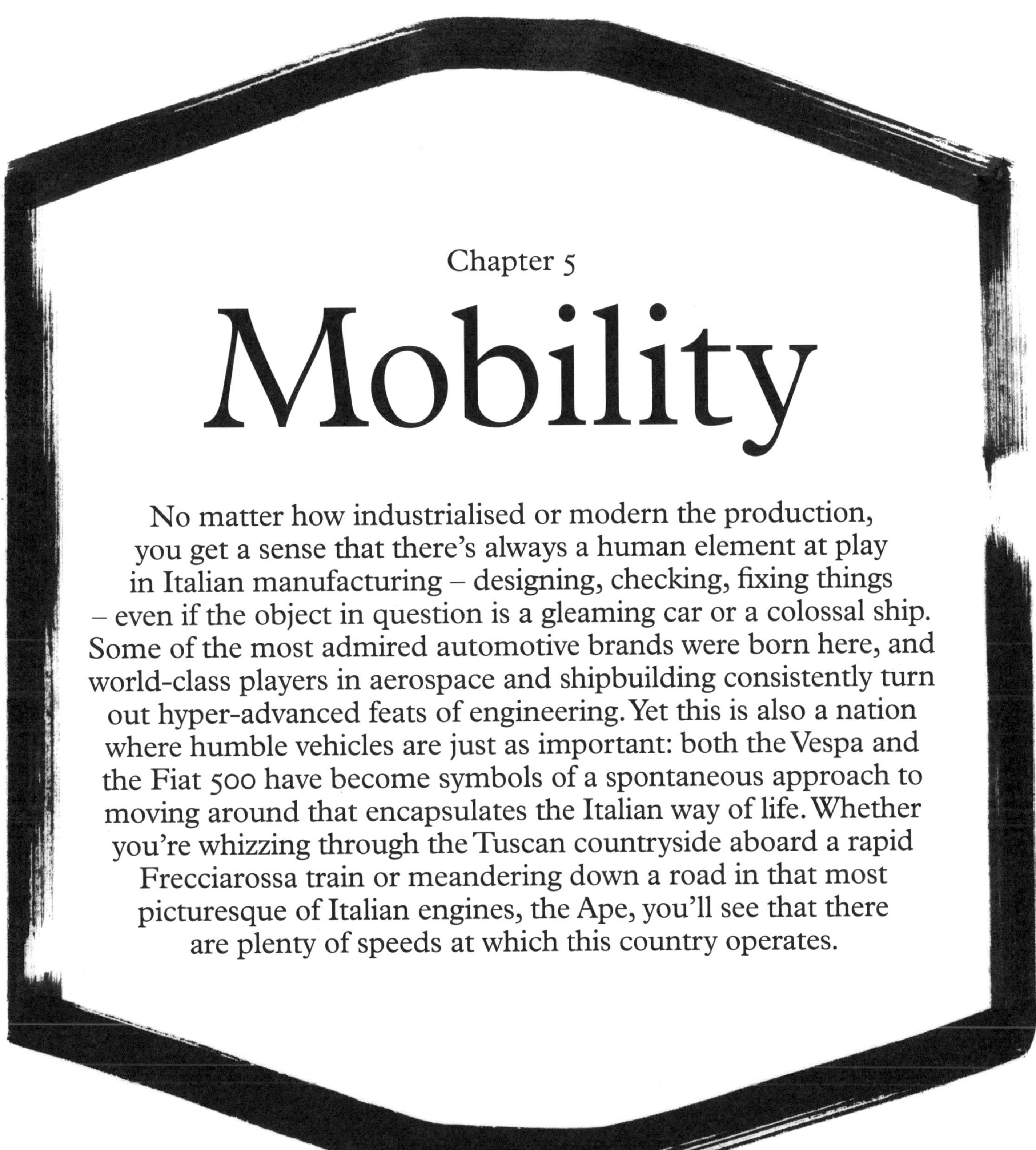

Chapter 5

Mobility

No matter how industrialised or modern the production, you get a sense that there's always a human element at play in Italian manufacturing – designing, checking, fixing things – even if the object in question is a gleaming car or a colossal ship. Some of the most admired automotive brands were born here, and world-class players in aerospace and shipbuilding consistently turn out hyper-advanced feats of engineering. Yet this is also a nation where humble vehicles are just as important: both the Vespa and the Fiat 500 have become symbols of a spontaneous approach to moving around that encapsulates the Italian way of life. Whether you're whizzing through the Tuscan countryside aboard a rapid Frecciarossa train or meandering down a road in that most picturesque of Italian engines, the Ape, you'll see that there are plenty of speeds at which this country operates.

Cars, trains and planes:
Power trip

Though they might not be best known for punctuality in their personal lives, Italians know how to move with speed and pizzazz. The engineering know-how within their vehicles is always paired with a penchant for comely appearances – be it a supercar's aerodynamic lines, the pointy nose of a high-speed train or some well-appointed airline liveries.

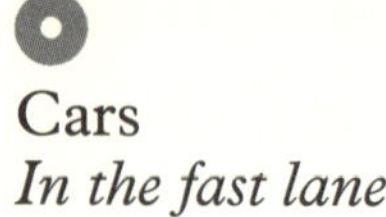

Cars
In the fast lane

German cars are known for their reliability, American cars for utility but people buy Italian cars for their design. The world's most extravagant supercars are made by the country's marques, many of which can be found based in the northern region of Emilia-Romagna. Its standing as the global home of supercar production has earned itself the nickname "motor valley".

Synonymous with speed thanks to its longstanding investment in Formula 1 racing, Ferrari and its iconic prancing black stallion logo and signature red livery has attracted legions of fans over the years. The seductive and superfast models are only matched by the high-performance examples from rival Lamborghini. Known for its attractive range of two-door coupés and convertibles, such as the Huracán, Lamborghini creates vehicles with aggressive lines and characteristic swing-up door design.

Modena-based Maserati, however, draws on its century of experience to lure enthusiasts. The brand continues to revamp popular models such as its luxury Quattroporte sedan as well as introduce newer models including its GranTurismo touring vehicle, mid-size Ghibli sedan and Levante SUV.

But it's not just the sporty types that can get their engines going when it comes to Italian brands: the Fiat group (which also includes the high-power Alfa Romeo) produces some of the nation's most ubiquitous cars. From Puntos to Pandas or the prolific 500, almost every Italian family has had a Fiat in their garage at some point.

Trains
Full speed ahead

The introduction of the high-speed network Frecciarossa has completely transformed the reputation of Italian trains, long mocked for their inconsistencies, slow pace and frequent delays. Arguably one of Europe's best high-speed offerings, it has revolutionised the country's mobility – many journeys that once required a night train can now be done in less than a day.

Italy's state railway operator Trenitalia launched its Freccia system in 2009. A massive infrastructure investment, it introduced mostly elevated tracks that connected Milan, Turin and Venice, with Rome and Naples linked via Florence and Bologna. The scarlet-hued Frecciarossa 1000 is built by Hitachi Rail Italy in Pistoia while a clutch of stations designed by architects including Santiago Calatrava and Zaha Hadid add to the experience.

Overall, Italy is a high-speed success: passengers on Trenitalia high speed trains rose from 6.5 million in 2008 to 40 million in 2018. And that doesn't count the trips taken on its rival – the equally sleek Italo launched in 2012 by what was Europe's first private high-speed train service.

Alitalia
Founded in 1947 as Italy's national flag carrier, Alitalia hasn't had the easiest ride since the dawn of the new millennium. Its company HQ and global hub at Rome's Fiumicino Airport has all too often received – and pushed out – new investors, administrators, and government representatives with bail-out cheques.

Business and profitability aside (although it should be noted that it has been voted one of Europe's most punctual airlines), it is Alitalia's classic mid to late-20th-century design that makes it stand out. Back in 1947, the firm cleverly gave itself the portmanteau of Alitalia: *ali* being the Italian word for wings, creating its punchy "Wings of Italy" name.

In 1967, graphic designer Walter Landor was brought in for a rebrand that spoke of professionalism, modernity – and was unmistakably Italian. The stylised Helvetica font exudes a refined nature while the racing green stripe adds an element of sporty chic. Adaptations over the years have more or less retained Landor's vision of the Italian jet age. But it's not just the branding that's enjoyed a remodel or two. Well-known for its designer attire, Alitalia's cabin crew uniforms have been conceived by some of Italy's most sought-after designers. The 1990s saw Giorgio Armani transform the look with a masculine double-breasted blazer while Mila Schön's 1969 emerald mini skirts and thigh-high boots combo – the outfit completed with a runway-ready cape – was a particularly glitzy affair.

Like a cat with nine lives, Alitalia has bounced back time and again – it was completely taken over by the state in March 2020. But through it all, there is one constant: it carries the prestigious title of being the Pope's airline of choice.

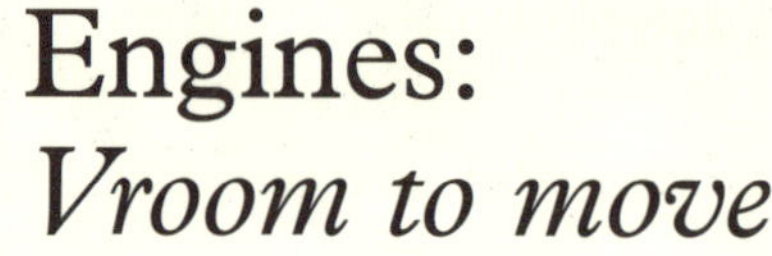

Engines:
Vroom to move

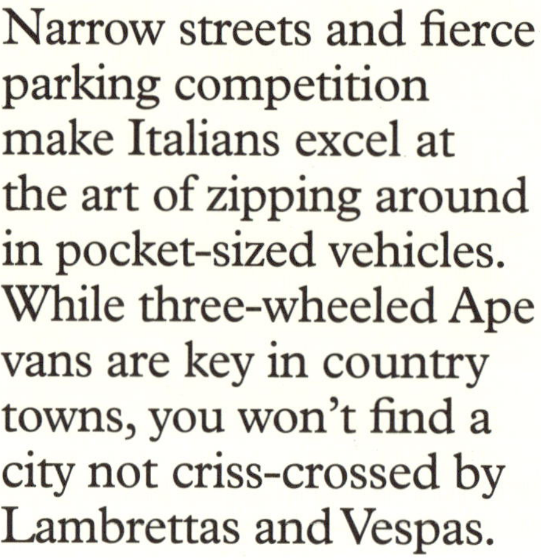

Narrow streets and fierce parking competition make Italians excel at the art of zipping around in pocket-sized vehicles. While three-wheeled Ape vans are key in country towns, you won't find a city not criss-crossed by Lambrettas and Vespas.

Pedals:
On your bike

For all the hasty drivers, there's a whole other gear to Italy's thoroughfares. Whether clad in Lycra or Prada, Italians have perfected the art of looking good on two wheels, and are proof that sometimes it pays to slow down a notch.

Boats and bikes:
Coasting along

This nautical nation has maintained a particular aptitude for making vessels – these days, not only of the seafaring sort, but the holiday-making kind too. Back on land, even the humble bicycle has its own high-end producers.

Small boats
All aboard

Given the country's 7,000km of coastline and countless scenic spots at which to drop anchor, it comes as no surprise that Italians are partial to messing about on the water. Luckily the nation is home to an armada of boatmakers where some still manufacture old-school wooden boats by hand while others excel at building speedy runabouts.

Ligurian builder Toy Marine offers a revamp of the classic lobster boat while Bluegame Yachts makes sleek utility vessels that provide plenty of deck space for sunbathing or sport fishing. And despite having been taken over by a Chinese company in 2012, the legendary boatmaker Riva is still the bearer of unmistakable Italian aesthetic – as per its classic model, the Aquarama.

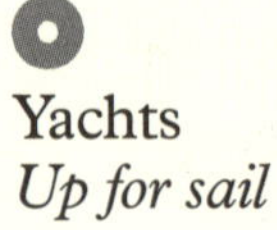

Yachts
Up for sail

All the way down the Ligurian and Tuscan coast, the Italian Riviera is dotted with marinas and the boatyards that keep them full of shiny new models. Unsurprisingly, what makes yachts popular is not just their engineering prowess but their elegant design too. Italian yacht builder Sanlorenzo, which has chartered a precise course in creating a portfolio of luxury pleasure crafts, has partnered with leading furniture brands – including kitchen-maker Boffi and lighting firm Artemide – to make life onboard as comfortable and attractive as on *terraferma*.

Others with a sizeable backlog of orders and a wide range of models include Tuscan-based Azimut and Perini Navi, both well-known for majestic sailing yachts. Another of the most prolific producers is the Ferretti Group, which oversees brands such as Wally, known for its innovative hull designs that have made waves within the industry.

Ships
Ferry impressive

Few nations possess the ability and resources to both commission the building of an aircraft carrier *and* complete the work on one. Italy is part of that select club thanks to Trieste-based firm Fincantieri. The multibillion-euro company operates several shipyards around the pensinsula, which are capable of producing a portfolio of warships that extend from littoral combat crafts and frigates to submarines.

Those same boatyards are equally able to handle orders from high-net-worth individuals looking to commission designs for luxury megayachts. If that weren't enough, its facilities are at the service of leading cruise operators too. Over the years, Fincantieri's manufacturing sites have launched numerous passenger ferries and some of the world's biggest cruise ships.

And its impressive industrial expertise has been called on for building efforts on land, as the accomplished company was one of the key partners in helping to erect the Renzo Piano-designed bridge in Genoa to replace a fallen structure in 2018. Fincantieri is yet to prove there's something it can't do.

Bikes
Pedal pushers

Racers around the world know that Italian-made bikes are some of the best around and the tradition of building them goes way back. Founded in Milan in 1885, Bianchi is the world's oldest bicycle manufacturer – it pioneered the use of equal-sized wheels with pneumatic rubber tyres. Its range of racing, all-road and endurance models, often enshrined in its signature celeste green, still possess a somewhat vintage charm – despite its high-end offerings being snapped up by top competitors.

In Treviso, premium maker Pinarello is famed for its high-performance frames used by athletes in competitions ranging from the Tour de France to the Olympics, while the brand's mountain bikes kit out weekend enthusiasts who enjoy a challenging ride. But leisurely city cyclists can count on a plethora of smaller-scale makers too – including Abici – many of which still honour a retro look.

Chapter 6

Meet the people

Fiery, chatty and effusive: Italians are almost conditioned by society to become extroverts. Plenty of strong characters are to be found in every profession – their self-assurance always appreciated. Over the past few centuries Italians have emigrated around the world, exporting their ebullience and sometimes becoming international household names in the process. True to their commitment to family businesses, their surnames are often brand names in themselves – yet more proof that they aren't shy of getting personally involved and invested in their enterprises. From singers to architects, directors to chefs, here is our gallery of the individuals helping to make a name for the nation today.

Mahmood
Pop star
Alessandro Mahmoud (stage name Mahmood) was born in Milan to an Italian mother and Egyptian father. His lyrics, which address his mixed heritage, have sparked conversations about what it means to be Italian today. In 2019, his win of the music competition at the Sanremo Music Festival made waves in the nation's cultural scene: his mesmerising hit "*Soldi*" went on to win second place at the Eurovision Song Contest the same year.

Lilli Gruber
Journalist
Bolzano-born TV host Lilli Gruber's striking combination of glamour and fearlessness has made her *Otto e Mezzo* talk show Italy's best arena for grilling politicians. While a gig as a foreign correspondent led her to report from Berlin, Iraq and Israel, her longest absence from the presenter's chair was due to a four-year stint as an MEP when, as an independent candidate for a centre-left coalition, she beat Silvio Berlusconi to the post in 2004.

Giuseppe Sala
Politician
Milan has Giuseppe Sala to thank for its transformation into the cosmopolitan hotbed of activity and investment it is now. A one-time corporate executive, Sala was elected mayor in 2016 and set about dedicating his business acumen to long-term projects that helped improve Milan's urban mobility. He also counts securing the 2026 Winter Olympic Games for Milan Cortina among his many accolades.

Patrizia Sandretto Re Rebaudengo
Art collector
Some of the best contemporary art spaces in Italy are helmed by private collectors who are publicly minded. One of the finest can be found in Turin, belonging to Patrizia Sandretto Re Rebaudengo who turned her passion for art into a career when she established the Fondazione Sandretto Re Rebaudengo in 1995. She is widely regarded as one of the world's most important collectors – and she has a pretty impressive selection of necklaces too.

Roberto Saviano
Author
Shining a light on Italy's murky underworld has made Saviano both a respected literary figure and an incendiary mob target – he is forced to live under constant police protection. He's best known for *Gomorra*, his courageous 2006 exposé of the notorious Camorra criminal organisation, which has exercised tyrannical rule over the Campania region where he was raised. A film adaptation was released in 2008 (*see page 145*).

Ayomide Folorunso
Athlete
Hurdler Ayomide Folorunso is part of a new generation of Italian athletes. Born in Nigeria and raised in the town of Fidenza in Emilia-Romagna, she was a semifinalist at the Rio Olympic Games where she set the Italian record at the 4x400m relay. Off the track, she's a medical student and aspiring pediatrician at the University of Parma.

Michele De Lucchi
Architect and designer
Bushy-bearded De Lucchi is an icon of Italian design who refuses to be defined by a particular medium. A trained architect, he began his career working for furniture manufacturer Kartell before meeting Ettore Sottsass, joining Studio Alchimia and becoming a founding member of the Memphis Group. His decades-long career has seen him design everything from Alessi coffee pots to a bridge in Tbilisi.

Angela Missoni
Creative director
After taking over the family business in 1997, Angela Missoni set about reinvigorating her parents' storied fashion label with a modern cosmopolitanism that placed it firmly back in the zeitgeist. She's responsible for elevating the company into a global luxury brand known around the world for its technicolour zigzag fabrics that are still produced in the textile mills of northern Italy.

Paolo Sorrentino
Film director
Sorrentino's films chronicle the splendour (and squalor) of Italy's high bourgeoisie and are celebrated worldwide for their keen-eyed cinematography and intimate portrayals of haunted heroes. Born in Naples, he made his directorial debut in 2001 with *One Man Up* before cementing his international recognition with *The Consequences of Love* (2004), which paved the way for Oscar-winner *The Great Beauty* (2013).

Rossana Orlandi
Gallerist
When the international design community descends on Milan for Salone del Mobile every spring, Rossana Orlandi's space is inevitably the first stop. Orlandi, who is rarely to be seen without her oversized sunglasses, opened her own shop-cum-gallery in 2002 with the aim of showcasing emerging talent. It has become Italy's premier destination for spotting the rising stars of the design world.

Stella Jean
Fashion designer
The only black member of Italy's chamber of fashion, Stella Jean has become the leader of a movement that calls for greater diversity in the industry. Her eponymous clothing brand, which launched in 2011 after she won *Vogue Italia*'s prestigious "Who Is On Next?" competition, collaborates with craft communities around the world to create pieces with bright prints and details from sustainable materials.

Massimo Bottura
Chef
Arguably Italy's best – and certainly its most internationally celebrated – chef Massimo Bottura opened Osteria Francescana in his hometown of Modena in 1995. The restaurant's menu features Bottura's own playful spin on traditional Italian cuisine and won him a three-star Michelin rating in 2011. Bottura and his wife Lara Gilmore established Food for Soul in 2016, a non-profit organisation that uses supermarket waste stock to create meals for the homeless and vulnerable at numerous *refettori* (community kitchens) around the world.

Chapter 7

Hospitality

The global popularity of Italian restaurants can be attributed to more than a mere appreciation of the country's delicious food. There's a familiarity to these establishments that makes them so special. You'll often find an enveloping warmth to both the people in the kitchen and the dishes on the menu. Italian cuisine is humble, comforting and often disarmingly simple, built around the staples of tomato, cheese, pasta and bread. Everything rests on the quality of these ingredients – little skill is needed if all that's necessary for the perfect lunch is a slice of mozzarella drizzled with olive oil. Whether in a hotel or *trattoria*, there's a high chance that the people who greet you at the door are working in their family business and it won't be long before you are welcomed into the fold. Eating, drinking and staying the night are all about conviviality: an old-school way to build powerful ties.

Eating out:
In good taste

From a brioche for breakfast and a sit-down lunch that often involves more than one course, to a quick pizza in the evening, Italians float in and out of cafés, restaurants and bars throughout the day. While there are countries where showing up to a restaurant unannounced is risky, most Italians live their daily culinary life with a dose of spontaneity. Warm hosts – many of whom treat waiting as a lifelong career rather than a part-time job – are usually happy to whip out the white tablecloth late into the night if you show up with an appetite.

This relaxed approach may have something to do with the fact that hitting a dud – tourist traps of Venice, Florence and Rome aside – is hard to do. In Italy, serving above-average, delicious food is the norm, not the exception. Often the most unassuming places hold the biggest surprises.

That much of its hospitality offering is made up of casual *trattorie* may also be the reason why fine dining is not as popular here as abroad. Traditional recipes are adhered to with respectful orthodoxy, which hasn't encouraged experimentation. Seeking out the best meals in humble locales is something of a national point of pride – and a quest that reaps plentiful rewards.

What to order: *Step up to the plate*

Beyond the country-wide staples of pasta and pizza, there are many speciality dishes that are fiercely tied to regional identity and others that only appear on tables at certain times of the year. Here's our menu of highlights – and where to order them.

Olive all'ascolana
A street food popular in Marche, these meat-stuffed, breaded olives are often served in paper cones.

This snack's name translates as "little oranges"

Arancine
A Sicilian delicacy of crispy fried rice balls stuffed with everything from ham and cheese to ragù and peas.

Farinata
This Ligurian pancake-like bake is made from just three ingredients: chickpea flour, water and olive oil.

Panzanella
Day-old bread is rehydrated with a dressing of tomato juice, vinegar and olive oil in this Tuscan salad.

Piadina
Stuffed with all manner of fillings and folded in half, this Emilia-Romagna flatbread dates back to the 1300s.

Carciofi alla giudia
A dish originally from Rome's Jewish quarter, the artichokes are fried until crisp on the outside and tender within.

Pappa al pomodoro
A favourite in Tuscany, this tomato soup is made using stale or leftover bread and topped with fresh basil.

Wood-fired pizza ovens can reach temperatures of up to 500C

Pizza margherita
Named and popularised after Queen Margherita of Savoy, it was presented to her on her first visit to Naples.

Bagna cauda
Translated as "hot bath", this sauce from Piedmont is served fondue-style and made with anchovies and garlic.

Ribollita
This hearty Tuscan stew is filled with cannellini beans, kale and chunks of bread and served with parmesan.

Risotto alla Milanese con ossobuco
Braised veal shin complete with bone marrow is served atop a rich saffron risotto in this Lombardy dish.

Pasta e ceci
A wholesome Roman stew consisting of pasta and chickpeas cooked in a warming tomato broth.

Cacio e pepe
Traditionally served with tonnarelli pasta, this sauce combines cheese and pepper with starchy pasta water.

Trofie al pesto
Twisted Ligurian pasta is cooked with potato cubes and green beans, and served with a zesty, fresh pesto.

Spaghetti vongole e bottarga
A zingy plate of spaghetti topped with clams and shavings of *bottarga* (cured fish roe) best enjoyed on the beach.

Pasta all'arrabbiata
The name of this Roman tomato sauce translates as "angry" in reference to its spicy kick.

Canederli or knödel
These bread dumplings from Italy's north are flavoured with cured meat and served in soup or with butter.

Ravioli al plin
The pinching technique used to seal these parcels of fresh pasta is what gave the Piedmontese dish its name.

Orecchiette alle cime di rapa
Small ear-shaped pasta is served with broccoli rabe, anchovies and red chilli in this Puglian classic.

These potato dumplings owe their ridges to the forks used to make them

Gnocchi al ragù
Inspired by the French *ragout*, this meaty sauce has many iterations with Bolognese its most famous.

Tortellini in brodo
This pork-filled pasta is another speciality of Bologna and comes in a clear chicken broth.

Gnocchi alla Romana
Unlike regular gnocchi, this Roman variety is made using semolina and is baked rather than boiled.

Polenta concia
A dish fit for mountain hikers from Valle d'Aosta, it involves a generous mix of polenta, cheese and butter.

Melanzane alla parmigiana
Fried slices of aubergine are layered with tomato sauce and parmesan in this baked delight.

Minestrone
Cooked in stock, this thick soup is made of pasta and whichever vegetables are in the cupboard.

Saltimbocca alla Romana
Veal escalopes are wrapped with prosciutto and sage before being marinated in wine and fried.

An entire bottle of wine is used for this recipe – *salute*!

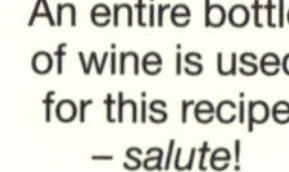

Brasato al Barolo
This melt-in-the-mouth Piedmontese main involves a joint of beef braised in the region's Barolo wine.

Cacciucco
Conceived in the Tuscan fish markets, this seafood stew is loaded with mussels, squid, octopus and prawns.

Cotechino e lenticchie
Eating boiled *cotechino* sausage with lentils is a New Year's Eve custom across Italy.

Vitello tonnato
A classic Piedmontese appetiser of sliced veal covered with a creamy tuna sauce and capers.

Baccalà mantecato
Salt cod is whipped with olive oil and served with polenta in this Venetian dish.

Arrosticini
These Abruzzese lamb skewers are traditionally cooked on a brazier called a *fornacella*.

Impepata di cozze
A classic Neapolitan antipasto of steamed mussels cooked with a generous helping of black pepper.

Sarde a beccafico
Baked sardines stuffed with raisins, pine nuts and breadcrumbs are a Sicilian favourite.

Panforte
Central Italy's answer to panettone, it comprises dried fruits and nuts glued together with molten sugar.

Babà al rum
Originating in France, these rum-soaked cakes were adopted by Neapolitans in the 19th century.

Zabaione
Egg yolks, sugar and sweet wine (often marsala) are whipped together to create this custard-like treat.

Seadas
These deep fried Sardinian pastries are filled with pecorino and lemon zest and served drizzled with honey.

These treats are also known as *chiacchere* or *frappe* in certain regions

Bugie
Traditionally made to celebrate carnival, these sweet fritters are served coated in sugar.

Cantucci e Vin Santo
In Tuscany these crunchy, twice-cooked almond biscuits are served with sweet dessert wine for dunking.

Baci di dama
Meaning "lady's kisses", these chocolate-filled hazelnut biscuits originated in the city of Tortona.

Affogato al caffè
This dessert's name (it translates as "drowned") refers to the scoop of vanilla ice cream doused in espresso.

Tiramisu
Rumour has it this pudding (its name means "pick me up") was invented in Treviso's 19th-century brothels.

Granita con brioche
A freshly baked brioche bun served with granita (crushed, flavoured ice) is a popular Sicilian breakfast.

Cannoli
These tubes of crisp, fried pastry are piped full of sugary ricotta. They are a staple Sicilian sweet treat.

Raisin-less pandoro is this bake's festive cousin

Panettone
Originally Milanese, this raisin and candied fruit-stuffed sweet bread is an integral part of Italian Christmas.

Eating in:
Home sweet home

An unmissable appointment for Sunday lunch at grandma's house is just the apex of a series of traditions that are aimed at getting people together around a table. However much they might enjoy meals out, most Italians fancy themselves as amateur chefs – many of them custodians of family recipes involving minuscule but all-important variations on time-honoured classics. (It goes without saying that each purports their nonna's to be the *best* version of lasagne.)

The idea of eating dinner at separate times – or worse still, in front of the TV – is anathema. There's something semi-sacred to setting the cutlery, taking a seat and focussing without distractions on the food and company. Huge bowls of pasta sitting at the table's centre – tagliatelle raised in slippery forkfuls before being deposited onto plates – are at the core of this big-hearted conviviality.

Even mid-week meals are prepared with creativity and panache; an invitation to somebody's house for supper is an occasion for the host to show off the best from their repertoire. Compliments are to be awarded plentifully while enormous second helpings should always be accepted readily as what they are: declarations of love. Abundance goes hand in hand with affection.

Food retailers:
What's in store

The bounty of produce yielded by this fertile land is sold by retailers that treat prosciutto, tomatoes and wheels of cheese with the reverence they deserve. Skip the supermarket and head to these small shops instead – you'll find a friendly smile behind the counter, too.

Volpetti
Rome

Umbrian brothers Claudio and Emilio Volpetti set up shop in 1973 in Testaccio, a Roman district renowned for its gastronomy. The deli spans the flavours of Italy, its shelves stacked with every imaginable variety of pasta, olive oil and balsamic vinegar. Thick legs of ham hang over the counter where white-aproned grocers stand ready to slice smoky *prosciutto di Praga* and *guanciale* (pork cheek) to order.

Provenance is an important part of the deli's dutifully selected offering, as is maintaining good relationships with producers – such as the Marfuga family, whose delectable olive oil has been stocked since Volpetti opened. An important neighbourhood mainstay, it becomes packed around lunchtime with locals eager to pick up hefty slices of *pizza ripiena*, a long tranche of focaccia dough stuffed with cheese and ham.

I Fruttarelli
Genoa

Shopping in Italy is a personal affair with many still choosing to buy their necessities from small, family-run businesses such as Genoa's I Fruttarelli – a fruit-and-veg vendor run by brothers Maurizio and Luciano Balossino.

"Everybody knows us and stops for a chat," says Maurizio, who delivers groceries using a three-wheeled Piaggio Ape van when not discussing the city's football clubs with passers-by.

The shop – its name a portmanteau of *frutta* (fruit) and *fratelli* (brothers) – opened in the 1980s and has served the community since, with the pair keeping tabs on odd behaviour and delivering goods to elderly customers. They rise before dawn to buy local produce, bringing back crates of plums and Ligurian squash. Foragers meanwhile gather mushrooms, reporting back to Luciano who takes the call on the old analogue phone next to the till.

Macelleria Annunciata
Milan

The Milanese know a thing or two about recognising a good cut – and not just when it comes to fashion. Mauro Brun opened his butcher shop Macelleria Annunciata in 1996 just steps from some of the city's most exclusive boutiques.

"Our philosophy is that when you eat, make it quality. People may not consume as much meat today but a good steak is one of life's finer pleasures, like wearing a good suit," says Brun. The cuts sold here come from a Piedmontese breed known for tasty and tender meat and Brun encourages customers to try lesser-known choices. For those cooking traditional fare, there are meatballs and *cotoletta alla Milanese* (breaded veal cutlet).

Pur Südtirol
Merano

The brainchild of two local entrepreneurs, Pur Südtirol aims to reintroduce old values to the supermarket industry. "We wanted to offer fair and pure products from regional farmers and become a platform for their goods," says co-owner Ulrich Wallnöfer who launched the burgeoning chain in 2010 with Günther Hölzl. The duo's first store was in their hometown of Merano and they have since opened branches in four other neighbouring towns.

Local and seasonal produce is a key element for the business, which is set up as a modern farmers' market where customers can taste and explore new goods in a welcoming space conceived by Tyrolean designer Harry Thaler. Almost half of the offering is organic and all items are sourced from South Tyrol, including juices from Karl Luggin and preserves from Partschillerhof.

Food markets:
Fare game

Since ancient times, Italy's vibrant food markets have formed the beating heart of the country's culinary life. Every small town and city neighbourhood has its own *mercato alimentare* with stands of fruit, vegetables, cheeses and meats proffered in a singsong sales pitch – a tradition upheld since the hawkers' choruses arrived with the Arabs in 800AD.

In Palermo's Ballarò market the historic roots are visible as well as audible, with twisting lanes lined with stands of produce and street food, just as it was when Arab travel writer Ibn Hawqal documented it in his journal 1,100 years ago. In Rome, the Campo de' Fiori bustles with well-coifed *signore* and eager home cooks jostling for the best tomatoes of the season.

The birth of a united Italy brought with it a flurry of covered markets erected across the nation, embodying the importance of these features of local life. Many of them still host the cities' markets and many more fill *piazze* weekly.

Where other nations depend on industrial agriculture, Italy's markets have maintained its ties to the fertility of the peninsula, keeping alive the demand for organice ingredients that define the country's cooking and relationship with food.

I NOSTRI
Limone
Latte Di mandorle
GRANITA D
LIMONE
2.00€
ORANGE
JUICE
SPREMUTA
D'ARANCIA
2.00€
Latte
di Mandorla
(Fresco)
Almond
Milk
(Fresh)
€ 1,50
Spremuta di
Arancia Bionda
Orange Juice
Spremuta di
Arancia Rossa
Red Orange Juice
Il Re della Granita
Il Re della Granita

The perfect pantry: *Shelf life*

A look inside an Italian kitchen cupboard reveals a world of packaging virtually unchanged for decades. These are the immutable essentials of the country's cuisine (with a few treats thrown in for good measure).

1.
Michele Portoghese bucatini pasta

2.
I Sapori di Corbara tinned tomatoes

3.
Pan di Stelle biscuits

4.
Sanbitter soft drink

5.
Campari aperitif

6.
Fratelli Contorno caponata sauce

7.
Don Antonio sauce

8.
Sai sea salt

9.
Tartufi Morra truffle oil

10.
Riso Riccò rice

11.
Lavazza coffee

12.
Mutti passata

13.
Cipriani bellini

14.
Ringo biscuits

15.
Palmera tinned tuna

16.
Pastiglie Leone pastille sweets

17.
Luglio olive oil

18.
Flott anchovies

19.
Punt e Mes vermouth

20.
Peroni beer

21.
Riseria Capittini rice

22.
Baci chocolates

23.
Pavesini biscuits

24.
Metelliana tinned cherry tomatoes

25.
Acqua Panna water

26.
Fabbri mint syrup

27.
Barbero chocolate bar

28.
Caffarel Gianduia chocolates

29.
Olio Barbera olive oil

30.
Narello artichoke hearts

31.
Ciomod chocolate bar

32.
Aperol aperitif

33.
La Grande Ruota polenta

34.
Star stock cubes

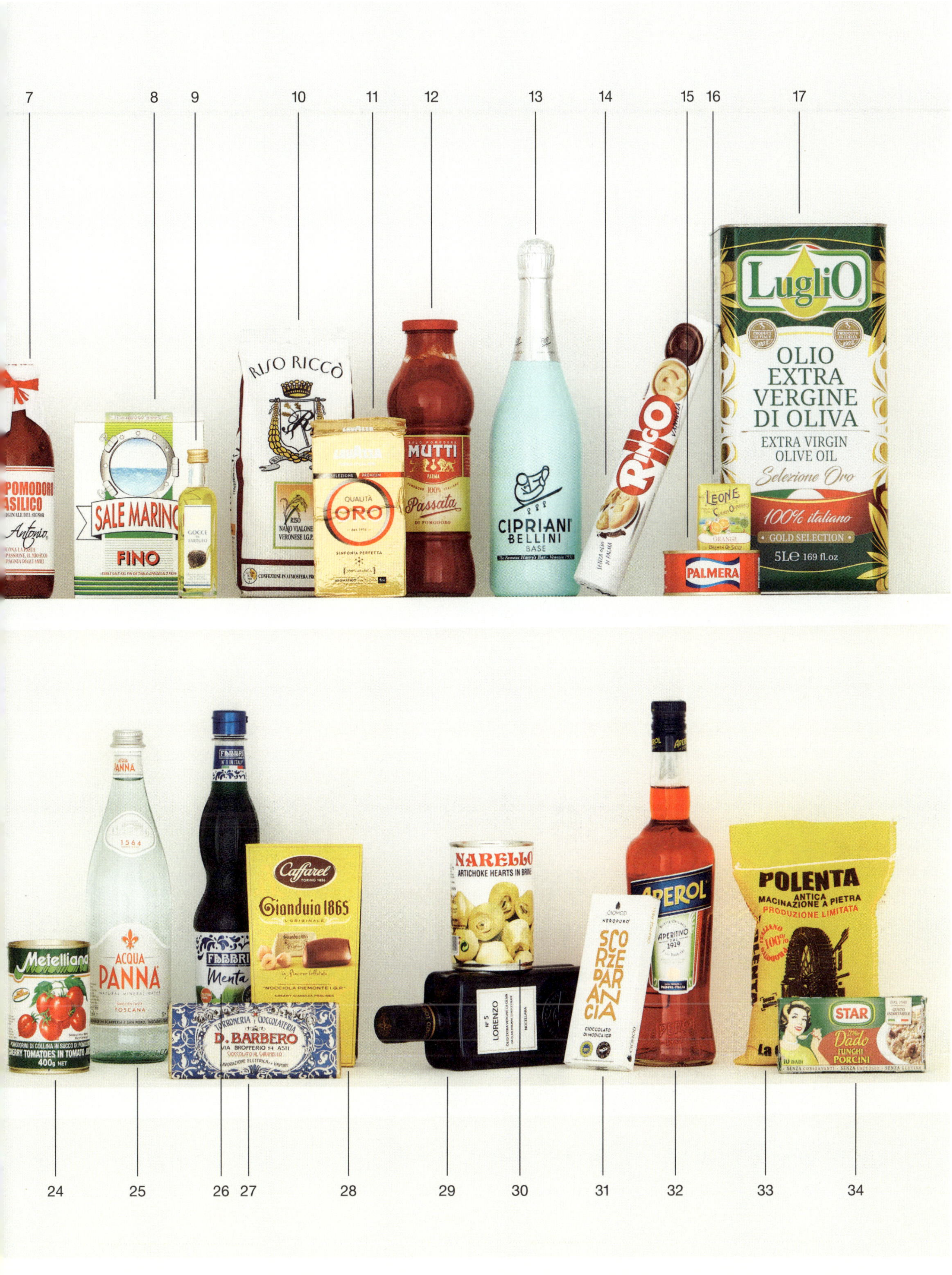
7
8
9
10
11
12
13
14
15
16
17
RISO RICCÒ
SALE MARINO
FINO
LAVAZZA
QUALITÀ ORO
MUTTI
Passata
CIPRIANI
BELLINI
BASE
RINGO
LEONE
PALMERA
LugliO
OLIO EXTRA VERGINE DI OLIVA
EXTRA VIRGIN OLIVE OIL
Selezione Oro
100% italiano
GOLD SELECTION
5L℮ 169 fl.oz
Metelliana
ACQUA PANNA
TOSCANA
FABBRI
Menta
Caffarel
Gianduia 1865
D. BARBERO
NARELLO
ARTICHOKE HEARTS IN BRINE
LORENZO
SCORZE DARANCIA
APEROL
APERITIVO
1919
POLENTA
ANTICA MACINAZIONE A PIETRA
PRODUZIONE LIMITATA
STAR
Dado
FUNGHI PORCINI
24
25
26
27
28
29
30
31
32
33
34

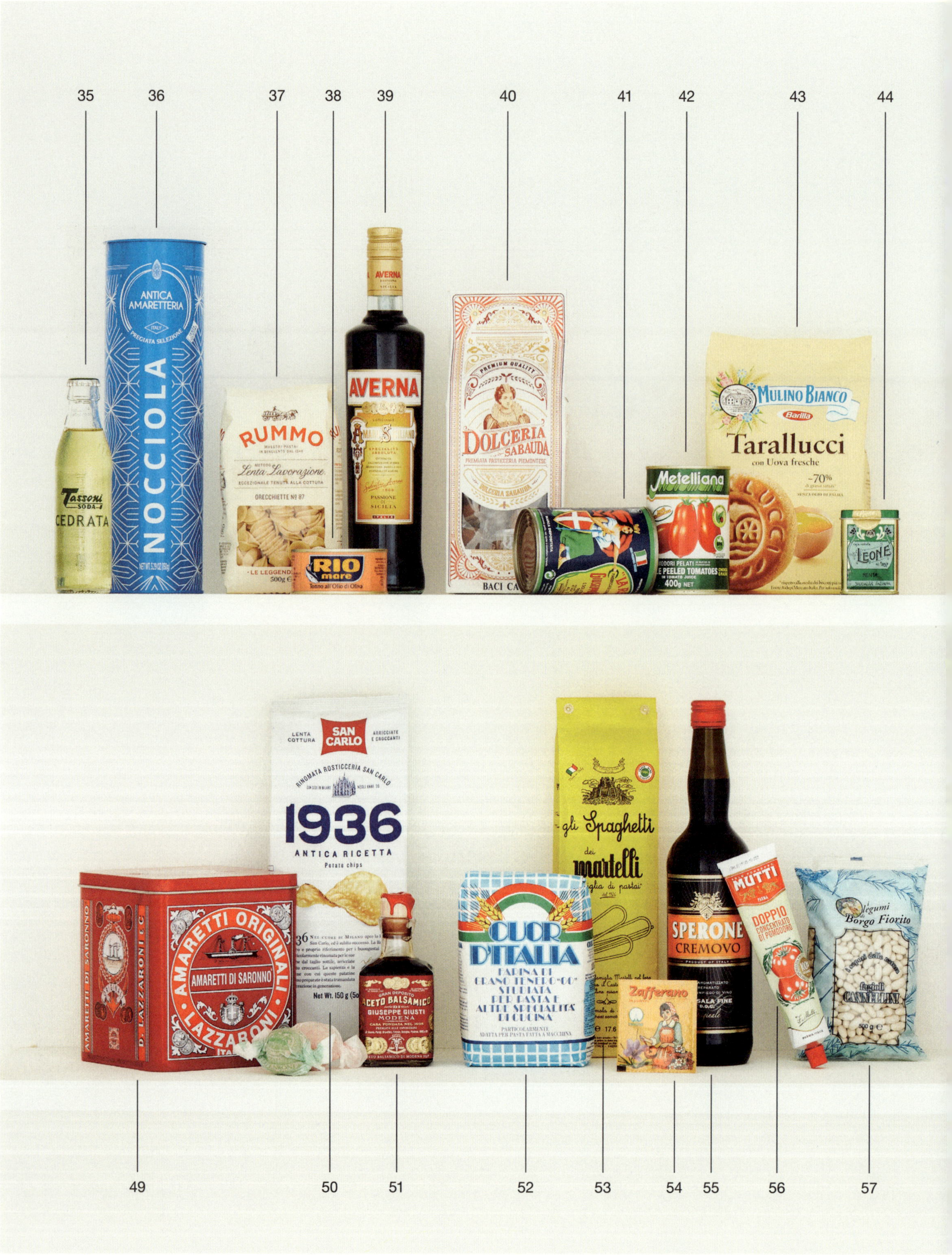
35
36
37
38
39
40
41
42
43
44
Tassoni
SODA
CEDRATA
ANTICA AMARETTERIA
NOCCIOLA
RUMMO
Lenta Lavorazione
RIO mare
AVERNA
DOLCERIA SABAUDA
PREMIUM QUALITY
Metelliana
MULINO BIANCO
Barilla
Tarallucci
con Uova fresche
LEONE
SAN CARLO
1936
ANTICA RICETTA
AMARETTI ORIGINALI
AMARETTI DI SARONNO
LAZZARONI
ACETO BALSAMICO
GIUSEPPE GIUSTI
MODENA
CUOR D'ITALIA
gli Spaghetti dei martelli
Zafferano
SPERONE
CREMOVO
MUTTI
DOPPIO CONCENTRATO DI POMODORO
Borgo Fiorito
fagioli CANNELLINI
49
50
51
52
53
54
55
56
57

35.
Tassoni soda

36.
Antica Amaretteria biscuits

37.
Rummo conchiglie rigate pasta

38.
Rio Mare tinned tuna

39.
Averna liqueur

40.
Dolceria Sabauda biscuits

41.
La Reale tinned tomatoes

42.
Metelliana tinned tomatoes

43.
Tarallucci biscuits

44.
Pastiglie Leone mint-flavoured pastille sweets

45.
Campari soda

46.
Duca di Sasseta chianti

47.
Angelo Parodi tinned tuna fillets

48.
Perbellini pandoro

49.
Lazzaroni amaretti

50.
San Carlo crisps

51.
Giuseppe Giusti vinegar

52.
Molino Spadoni flour

53.
Martelli spaghetti

54.
Pavone saffron powder

55.
Giacomo Sperone marsala

56.
Mutti tomato puree

57.
Borgo Fiorito cannellini beans

58.
Simmenthal tinned beef

59.
Faella penne pasta

60.
Chef cream

61.
Bepi Tosolini limoncello

62.
Capparis capers

63.
Cynar liqueur

64.
Fabbri cherries in syrup

65.
Michele Portoghese pasta

Food production: *Four case studies*

Italian cuisine may be one of the most beloved and widespread worldwide but it's not just a matter of good recipes and homely cooking. Food is big business: producing it to the scale that exports require (while maintaining all-important standards) is a huge undertaking. After all, as any Italian will tell you, the secret is in the quality of the ingredients.

Pasta
Mancini Pastificio Agricolo

Reportedly 63 per cent of Italians consume pasta every day and each family has their favourite brand, from De Cecco to Barilla. Today, one in three packets of pasta uses imported grains, but Massimo Mancini thinks there's a more sustainable way: "My aim is to make pasta the way we used to, under one roof." Launched in 2010, the brand's pasta is made from wheat grown on the family farm in Marche. Cut with bronze casts and air-dried for 45 hours, it offers not only a better flavour and nutritional value than its industrial counterparts but a lesser environmental impact too.

Coffee
Lavazza

With trade in more than 140 countries and 4,000 employees, it's hard to imagine that Lavazza began in a grocery shop in Turin. Luigi Lavazza founded the eponymous brand in 1895 and became known for his coffee blends. He roasted beans to enjoy at home, pioneering well-made packaging along the way.

Today, the family-run firm is continuing to evolve with a drive for sustainability: it launched The Lavazza Foundation in 2004 which supports coffee producing communities around the world and has published a Sustainability Report since 2014.

Nougat
Scaldaferro

A saccharine smell with a hint of vanilla fills the air in Scaldaferro's factory in Dolo, where bags of local almonds and hazelnuts fill the floor, soon to be mixed with honey from Sicily, Trentino and the Venetian lagoon to make the festive favourite of *torrone* (nougat).

Famously light and flaky, Scaldaferro's hand-moulded sweets are made using a recipe from the 1700s with sugar, egg whites, honey, vanilla and nuts. Italians have a taste for tradition, with *mandorlato classico* (with almonds) and *torrone morbido* (soft) still the best selling today.

Cheese
Hombre

Parmigiano-Reggiano is one of Italy's best-loved cheeses: in 2019 the country produced 150,000 tonnes – three million wheels worth €2.4bn – from just 450 licensed dairies. One of the few organic makers is Modena's Hombre. Each day, the dairy's 500 cows produce 7,000 litres of milk. Natural rennet is added to the milk and the curd broken up with a *spino* (whisk). It forms into a mass once heated and is placed into moulds and immersed in a brine. The wheels are left to mature for at least 12 months, with the strongest – the *Stravecchio* – up to 30.

Drink production:
Three case studies

Wine-making is so important to the Italian economy that vineyards are an integral part of the landscape. Each region has its own specialties and grapes which vary dramatically depending on terrain and climate. But it's not just about *rosso*, *bianco* and rosé – from craft beers to grappa and vermouth, there's plenty of entrepreneurial activity brewing across the boot.

Wine
Ferrari

In the age-old rivalry between Italian and French vineyards, sparkling wines are a hotly contested battleground. Where France has champagne, Italy has a number of denominations that answer to the title of *spumante*.

Trento-based Ferrari is one of Italy's most prestigious producers: it was founded in 1902 by Giulio Ferrari with the explicit intention of proving the country could make fine sparkling wines using the "traditional method" of in-bottle fermentation. Run by the Lunelli family since 1952, it makes 14 types of *spumante*, from rosé to demi-sec. Grapes are harvested from 500 environmentally conscious growers across the Dolomites, where the high-altitude soil and temperature variation give a mineral taste.

Grapes of worth
The world's biggest producer of wine, Italy has more than 350 official varieties. Generally, sweeter, fruitier kinds are found in the south while in the north they are crisper and more acidic. As well as big producers such as Antinori and Frescobaldi (whose origins date back to the 1300s) there is also a burgeoning natural wine scene that's quickly growing in acclaim. Here are a few of the bottles you'll find on our wine rack.

1.
Bianco O-X, Costadilà

2.
Ottavio Rube Rosso, Valli Unite

3.
Posca Bianca, Orsi

4.
Gavi, Tenuta San Pietro

5.
Alese, Tempo al vino

6.
Brut 25, Fratelli Berlucchi

7.
Tignanello, Marchesi Antinori

8.
Irpina Aglianico, Benito Ferrara

1

5

2

6

3

7

4

8

Beer
Forst

Despite being more naturally apt at making wine, Italy also has an interesting crop of breweries (perhaps linked to South Tyrol's proximity to its Mitteleuropean neighbours). Enter Forst: the family-run firm – named after the village where it was founded in 1857 – credits its taste to the mountain springs. "It's optimal because it's very pure," says brewmaster Christian Pircher, adding it's "just right" for making a variety of beers, aged for up to two months. Manager Cellina von Mannstein adds: "Beer matures for as long as it's needed. You can't rush quality."

Apéritif
Aperol

Concocted by the Barbieri family in Padua in 1919, Aperol was not an overnight success. Flavoured with bitter orange, rhubarb and other herbs and roots, the bright orange liqueur only started to achieve fame in the 1960s.

It soon entered the lexicon of bartenders, who mixed it with prosecco and soda water in a libation known as a spritz – which supposedly originated in the 19th century when beer-loving Austrian soldiers diluted wine with sparkling water. Particularly popular in Veneto, Aperol is now enjoying a boom well beyond Italy's borders.

Coffee:
Full of beans

Many countries can lay claim to having a world-class coffee culture but none can match Italy's as the birthplace of espresso. The sharp shot is the golden standard of all coffee orders here, which is why most refer to it as a *caffè normale*.

Despite a blissful ignorance (or purposeful avoidance) of flat whites, lattes and cortados, there are still countless variations in the way Italians order their coffees. Long, short, strong, creamy, macchiato (hot or cold): each person has their favourite. That's what makes a barista's knowledge of their regulars all the more important – when they show up for their morning fix, they need only ask for "*il solito, per favore*".

Like most specialities linked to Italian identity, there is a sense that there's a "right" and "wrong" way to consume coffee. Do drink however many you please: most people enjoy one at home, straight from their own moka pot. This solitary pleasure is often followed up with an espresso at the bar, sipped while engaging in friendly chatter. A quick shot is an omnipresent excuse for a break and a catch-up – and no meal is ever finished without one (including dinner, of course). Do remember you have to engage in the befuddling rigmarole of queueing for a ticket and paying in advance before queueing again at the counter. Don't even think about ordering cappuccino outside breakfast hours – and forget about takeaway. There's a reason espresso means fast: most people take theirs standing at the counter, all in one gulp, the sugar still crystallised at the bottom of the cup.

Bar Luce
Milan

A cross between a classic Italian bar and a scene plucked straight from *The Grand Budapest Hotel*, Fondazione Prada's Bar Luce was, of course, designed by director Wes Anderson. Kitted out with an old jukebox, vintage pinball machines and Formica-topped tables alongside the pastel hues that Anderson is famed for, the interior is sheer 1950s kitsch. But the highlight of it all? An old Faema coffee machine theatrically operated by mustachioed, bow tie-wearing waiters.

Caffè Al Bicerin
Turin

A Turinese stalwart since 1763, Caffè Al Bicerin made its name, quite literally, when its founder Giuseppe Dentis transformed the popular drink of the time, the *bavareisa*. A combination of coffee, cream and chocolate – or *n poc 'd tut* (a little bit of everything) – the *bicerin* has become a Piedmontese staple. Regulars seat themselves at one of the few tables within to enjoy the titular drink, homemade cakes and, at aperitivo, the café's bitter dark chocolate liqueur.

Orsonero Coffee
Milan

After noticing a gap in the market for speciality coffee, Canadian Brent Jopson and his Milanese wife, Giulia Gasperini, decided to shake things up by opening Orsonero. "We still sell more espressos than anything else but our customers are starting to cotton on to the flat white," says Jopson. "Filtered coffee is also popular though sometimes I have to explain it's not the same as an Americano." The pared-back, whitewashed space in the Porta Venezia area of Milan stands out from the rest of the city's coffee offerings.

Caffè Florian
Venice

The oldest café in Italy (it first opened its gilded doors in 1720), Caffè Florian on Venice's Piazza San Marco recalls a bygone era and has boasted presitigious patrons such as Dickens, Proust and Casanova in its time. Little has changed inside, where the rococo rooms are furnished with white marble tables, velvet banquette seating and panelled walls. The café prides itself on its *cioccolata con panna* (dark hot chocolate with whipped cream) – perfect for when the bora winter winds blow in.

Antico Caffè Torinese
Trieste

This art nouveau café was opened in 1919 by renowned Triestine artist and cabinetmaker Giuliano Debelli, who clad it from floor to ceiling in glossy teak panels and installed a vast crystal chandelier (which belies the café's diminutive size). By day, its marble bar is lined with locals sipping *capo in b* (macchiato in a glass). As night falls these are swapped for Negronis and vermouth-heavy *commistione* cocktails as the space transforms into one of the city's most popular watering holes.

Bar Mexico
Naples

Founded by Samuele Passalacqua in booming postwar Naples, Bar Mexico has three outposts in the southern city – and all of them are 1960s time-warps. Inside, baristas in vintage uniforms man original La San Marco machines to prepare Passalacqua's eponymous coffee brand, while locals stand at the mosaicked bars gossiping and knocking back piping hot *zuccherato* (sweetened) espressos and *harem con panna* (a velvety Arabica bean shot topped with thick cream).

Aperitivo:
A tipple or two

Lots of people enjoy a glass of wine at the end of the day but in Italy this indulgence is codified into aperitivo. Far from being an encouragement to excessive drinking, it's a way of "opening" somebody's appetite for dinner, which is why glasses of wine or light cocktails are always consumed with a little snack on the side. Despite the country's bounty of delicious wines and nibbles, Italians display a remarkable restraint over aperitivo.

That's because the point of this daily ritual isn't the wine but rather sharing it with a table of friends. It's a moment to unwind and offload the day's worries while enjoying bubbling conversation with a touch of decadence. Dating back to the Roman era, aperitivo typifies the epicurean talents of a country where drinking's goal is cheery relaxation and a satisfied stomach rather than drunkenness or frenzied abandon.

Whether a negroni *sbagliato* in Milan, a small *ombra* of wine in Venice or a Campari soda in Rome; be it ramekins of olives, a focaccia piled with tomatoes and cheese or *bruschette*, aperitivo comes in endless variants. But no matter where, at sundown the bars come alive with chatter and the clinking of glasses. *Cin cin!*

n'ombra de vin enoteca

Gelato:
What a scoop

Gelato isn't just ice-cream – the Italian version is churned slower (and with less cream) than its American cousin. It's also a year-round treat that's enjoyed by all. In August, it's not uncommon to see suited businessmen swapping lunch for a brightly hued three-flavour cone while no *passeggiata* (stroll) is complete without a gelato – true both for schoolkids on holiday and 20-year-olds on their way to the club.

For a recipe that involves only a handful of ingredients – water, sugar and pulp for fruity flavours, with the addition of milk and eggs for creamy versions – there is a mind-boggling number of variants. But the great classics – *crema, cioccolato, stracciatella* and *fior di latte* – remain unbeaten.

Gelato has a global history: it is said that the ancient Romans, Egyptians, Babylonians and Chinese enjoyed lapping on sweet snow concoctions and in 1686, a Sicilian opened the world's first *gelateria* in Paris. But over the centuries, it became an Italian affair: today, there are about 20,000 *gelaterie* in the country. With schools and a university training the makers of tomorrow, this artisanal tradition is far from being put on ice.

Hotels:
Suite dreams

If large hotel chains haven't always found a firm footing in the Bel Paese it's because the boot is dotted with independent inns that are run (often by dedicated families) with a charming, homely touch. From seafront marvels to mountain boltholes, here are the hoteliers to know.

Parco dei Principi
Sorrento

There are some hotels that draw a crowd for their architecture and design alone. Parco dei Principi is one. Designed by Gio Ponti and opened in 1962, the hotel overlooks the Mediterranean from its cliff-top spot on the edge of Sorrento.

Today, Ponti's vision remains unchanged with everything from the building's boxy structure to the textiles and majolica tiles still bearing his skilled touch. An elevator that descends through the stone cliff to a sunbathing jetty, restaurant and beach provides fairytale wonder.

"A hotel is not just a place where you sleep and eat – this place has character," says rooms division manager Fiorella Vecchia. "Ponti imagined it as a diamond set in the cliff, as a point in between the park and sea. That's what I think we need to represent too: a moment of pause, an experience that Ponti tried to express through this space."

Hotel Danieli
Venice

One of the most storied hotels in the city, as well as the setting for not one but *three* James Bond films, Hotel Danieli is a particularly grand affair. Comprising three *palazzi*, the oldest of which dates back to the 14th century, the address boasts 210 stately rooms – many of which overlook the lagoon.

Moments from the Ponte dei Sospiri (Bridge of Sighs), the entrance leads into a majestic lounge where guests relax on ruby red armchairs lit by Murano-glass chandeliers.

The first floor is home to the venue's largest suites, including the Doge Dandolo Royal which features an 18th-century fresco by Jacopo Guarana and a fireplace adorned with the Dandolo family's coat of arms. The hotel's most spectacular sight, however, is from the top floor Terrazza Danieli restaurant where the views of the Bacino di San Marco are breathtaking.

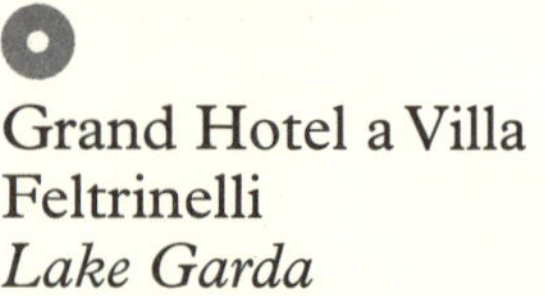

Grand Hotel a Villa Feltrinelli
Lake Garda

The grand hotel moniker is hard to live up to for many, but not Villa Feltrinelli. "We are a small but great hotel," says owner Markus Odermatt. Built in 1892 for the Feltrinelli family, the residence was confiscated during the Second World War by Benito Mussolini. Once retrieved by the family, it enjoyed many a bash before it was sold in 1997 and transformed into the residence it is today.

At the estate on the shores of Lake Garda, guests can enjoy the villa's palatial grounds planted with centuries-old magnolias and trees such as citrus, olive and fig. There are fresh herbs too, many of which end up in the restaurant's refined fare. "Our philosophy is not the same as a 'normal' hotel," says Odermatt. It's no wonder that vacancies for its 20 guestrooms and cottages are hard to come by.

Gasthof Bad Dreikirchen
Barbiano, South Tyrol

Renovated by Rome-based Lazzarini Pickering Architetti, the secluded Bad Dreikirchen hotel enjoys sweeping views down the Valle Isarco and some of the cleanest air in Europe.

Set on the hillside above the quaint village of Barbiano in South Tyrol, the building is over 600 years old and takes its name from the three ancient churches clustered on the historic Roman site. "The hotel takes you on a journey into the past: the rooms have no TVs but there is a well-stocked library," says Matthias Wodenegg, who runs the hotel with his wife Annette. "The panoramic view soothes the spirit and the scent of the forests and fields helps our guests get away from it all."

A 30-minute drive from Bolzano, the hotel's 26 rooms – all pine-clad in charming Tyrolean style and with their own balcony or loggia – make for a welcome Alpine retreat.

Masseria Moroseta
Ostuni, Puglia

Nestled within a five-hectare olive grove in the Puglian countryside, Masseria Moroseta is a modern haven. Part of a working farm that produces fruit, vegetables and olive oil – served up for breakfast with eggs fresh from the resident chickens – it has six rooms each with a garden or terrace.

Designer Andrew Trotter modelled the simple space on Puglia's traditional *masserie* (farmhouses), dotting the rooms around a central courtyard. Stone walls reflect those found in nearby Ostuni, named "The White City", which along with vaulted ceilings and stone floors keep the interior cool. An enclave of relaxation, guests can enjoy morning yoga and cooking lessons come sunset, with laps in the pool in between.

Chapter 8

Retail

It's one thing to know how to create a beautiful and enduring product but it's another to understand how to successfully bring it to market – fortunately, Italians know their way around a sales pitch. From the early Middle Ages, Italy established itself not only as a nation of manufacturers but of merchants too: the ships of Genoa, Pisa and Venice ruled the Mediterranean, exchanging goods of all kinds. Today, the best way to appreciate the art of Italian retail is to head to a small, specialist shop. Most owners have a knowledge of the products on their shelves that is nothing short of astonishing. Many become life-long confidants of their clients and are all too happy to administer advice and provide small fixes (often carried out for free) in the name of good, friendly service. Even in the glitziest locales, this personable approach remains: in Italy, a purchase is hardly ever a throwaway transaction.

Luxury fashion: *Club couture*

Italy has centuries of retail experience up its well-tailored sleeve (it's no coincidence that the Venetians invented the cheque) and has firmly established itself not only as the most respected and powerful producer of luxury fashion in he world, but also the master of selling it.

Visit Via Montenapoleone in Milan or Rome's Via Condotti and you'll find a roster of names synonymous with global style: Prada, Gucci, Giorgio Armani, Salvatore Ferragamo and more. Each brand has created dazzling temples of retail in gleaming marble and gold leaf where impeccable doormen greet customers and products are displayed with the reverence of high art.

A newer generation of brands such as Slowear and Sunnei has injected a more youthful vision into the country's sartorial scene, with sleek contemporary boutiques to match. But impressive spaces only go so far: personalised service remains the central selling point. Italy is proof that the recipe for a successful shop lies in good taste, pride in product and a highly passionate individual or two.

Clockwise from far left: inside Fendi's palatial Rome address; Gucci in Rome; a shopper passes Salvatore Ferragamo in Florence; Boglioli's Milanese outpost; all shop and no stop; Giorgio Armani in Milan; looking sharp at Tod's, Milan

Independent fashion:
One of a kind

Milan, Italy's well-turned-out fashion capital, is not the only place you'll find cutting-edge fashion. Second-tier cities – and even country towns – are home to progressive retailers that cater for a clientele that's anything but provincial.

Zoe
Bassano del Grappa

Cristina Crespina had worked for several fashion brands when she launched a small womenswear shop in Veneto's Bassano del Grappa in 1998. "People used to tell me I was crazy to open a boutique here," she says. "But I had to do something to my taste and others ended up liking it too."

In time, Crespina opened outposts in Pietrasanta in Tuscany and Sardinia's Porto Rotondo. But Bassano is where she still spends most of her time. Her presence makes all the difference when guiding customers through the riotously colourful collection of clothes. "It makes much more sense if I am there to explain, which is a mixed blessing," she laughs. From Forte Forte dresses to jumpsuits by Sara Roka, there's no room for plain on these shelves.

Eraldo
Ceggia

The Veneto town of Ceggia (population 6,000) is not the first place you'd expect to find a four-floor fashion mecca stocking more than 480 designers. Yet this is exactly where Eraldo set up shop, attracting customers with its selection spanning Gucci and Givenchy to cult designers including Japan's Sacai and South Korea's Juun J.

Launched in 1947 as a haberdashery that sold supplies in the wake of the Second World War, Eraldo shifted to clothing over the decades. By the 1990s, its popularity had its owners, the Ferrante family, questioning whether to relocate. Instead they upgraded the premises, building a minimalistic cube – its modern exterior only heightening the incongruity between the retailer and its surrounds. "Being so out of the way has meant we've tried to go beyond our own possibilities and raise the bar," says third-generation owner Alberto Ferrante (*pictured*).

Sugar
Arezzo

What began as a small boutique in the pint-sized Tuscan city of Arezzo in the 1980s has grown to become one of Italy's most trend-setting clothing shops. Beppe Angiolini's multi-brand shop now counts several locations around his hometown but its flagship occupies the city's Palazzo Lambardi.

Here, shoppers can find the latest designs by the likes of Valentino and Versace under carved wooden ceilings and between ornately frescoed walls. Alongside these Italian high-fashion behemoths, the shop also stocks more contemporary brands including Off-White and R13 together with a selection of books, magazines and homeware. There's also an on-site café-cum-cocktail bar called No Sugar Please and on the top floor you'll find Sugar Rooms – a chic 12-room hotel.

A Gi Emme
Como

This dapper clothes shop was opened in 1957 by Adriano and Mariella Monti. Owned today by their son Alberto, it provides its discerning clientele with understated tailoring and luxury Italian knitwear, with pieces from Massimo Alba, Incotex and Zanone.

From its position on the banks of Lake Como, the boutique aims its offering at affluent northern Italians for whom investment in high-quality fashion is a given. "We select the brands we carry based on traditional craftmanship with a focus on Italian quality," says Adriano Monti. Alberto adds: "I select local brands in every country; in Milan, I buy Aspesi and Golden Goose; in Paris, Vanessa Bruno and Repetto. I have private contacts in New York, Paris and Copenhagen. I also take photos in the street to capture special looks."

Specialists:
Ask the experts

In a world that's increasingly moving towards superstores that stock everything under the sun, Italians are remarkably committed to buying their goods from the place that's expert at making and selling them – often, from shops that are more workshop than retail space.

1.
Ferramenta Brugnara
Merano

South Tyrolean retailer Ferramenta Brugnara goes above and beyond the remit of the average hardware shop. From mattocks to mallets, it sells every imaginable tool and customers come from far and wide for advice and equipment to tackle their DIY quandaries. This one-stop-shop also stocks an extensive array of home and kitchenware, so you're just as likely to leave with a fondue kit as a fretsaw or set of keys.

2.
Drovetti
Turin

The Drovetti family woos passers-by with playful window displays of its most popular product: door handles. Inside are worn wooden counters that many a client has leaned on since it opened in 1916, all while discussing which lock to install or debating the ideal typeface for a door plaque. "Some furniture is even older than the shop," says Luigi Drovetti, revealing varying sizes of nails hidden within a 19th-century cabinet.

3.
Stay
Rome

In a city of chintzy linen shops, Stay stands out for its focus on fabrics. The brand was founded in 2015 by textile industry stalwart Ruben Fatucci and his partner Alessandra Azzali. Fatucci scours Italy for manufacturers who use natural fibres and dyes to create its sheets, towels, blankets, rugs and table linens in muted colours while Azzali is on hand inside the shop to help customers select the perfect linen for their homes.

4.
Gabriele Gmeiner
Venice

After stints with John Lobb in London and Hermès in Paris, Austrian shoemaker Gabriele Gmeiner moved to Venice to learn at one of the city's last ateliers. In 2003 she opened a workshop for bespoke footwear using calfskin from France, cordovan from Mexico and vegetable-tanned soles from Germany's Rendenbach. It takes 12 months from the first fitting to final product but it's well worth the wait.

5.
Ombrelli Maglia
Milan

Giorgio and Francesco Maglia's family has been in the umbrella-making business since 1854. The brand's bespoke designs are made in proportion to the buyer's height and arm length, with clients able to choose from an array of hand-carved handles made in woods ranging from hickory to hazelnut. Customers can also pick their preferred fabric for the awning, which is woven in the nearby city of Como.

6.
Drogheria Toso
Trieste

Little has changed since this historical drugstore was opened by Vittorio Toso in 1906. The walls are lined from floor to ceiling with large glass jars containing every imaginable filling from loose leaf tea and boiled sweets to bath salts and dried herbs – all of which is then packaged into paper bags and sold by weight. There is also a range of household items including ostrich-feather dusters and horsehair brooms on offer.

7.
Bruno
Venice

Since 2013, graphic designers Giacomo Covacich and Andrea Codolo have been creating branding for Venetian cultural institutions. In 2014 the studio started a new chapter: making and selling books. In its shop, art and design titles lie alongside fanzines and architecture tomes printed in their office. "It's a chance to show off books that combine interesting graphic design, content and quality of print," says Covacich.

8.
Officina Profumo-Farmaceutica di Santa Maria Novella
Florence

It may trade in luxury scents and handmade cosmetics today but this Florence pharmacy was founded in 1221 by monks who later produced disinfectants during the Black Death – making it one of the world's oldest pharmacies. It houses a small museum where visitors can view curiosities such as early books on the bubonic plague but its main draw is the building – a former chapel with vaulted ceilings, chandeliers and frescoes.

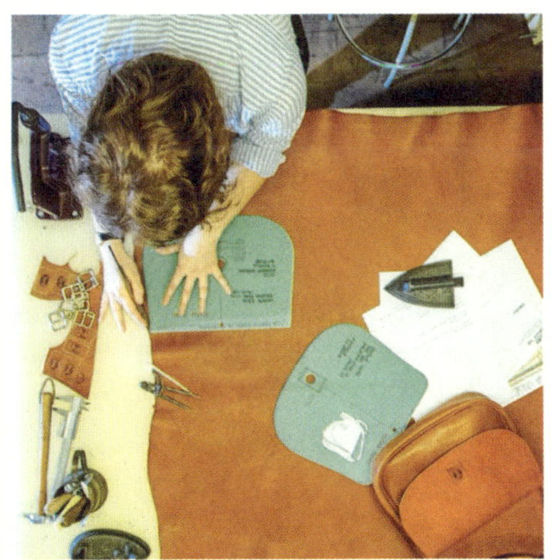

9.
La Vacchetta Grassa
Modena

With an abundance of spring-fed tanneries, it's no wonder Modena has been a centre for the Italian leather trade since the Middle Ages. And continuing the local craft is La Vacchetta Grassa, which occupies two floors of the 15-century Palazzo Barbanti Silva Bulli. Its ground-floor shop sells vegetable-tanned goods cut and stitched by hand in the workshop upstairs, using an unusual variety of materials including eel-skin and stingray.

10.
Rossignoli
Milan

Family-run Rossignoli started in 1900 as a classic *bottega*, a small workshop that sold bicycles made onsite. Today patrons queue below the old-school signage in the Brera district for the models, which are still welded, painted and assembled by craftspeople in Milan. "We adhere to the principles of Italian industrial design: it has to be beautiful, functional and at an accessible price," says owner Matia Bonato.

Mend and repair:
Can they fix it?

Perhaps it's because high-end manufacturing is a particular point of pride and the process of making remains close to home that Italians know and appreciate the time, money and effort that goes into producing everyday items. So it's not just a frugal disposition (inherited from an earlier generation that often struggled to make ends meet) that's behind a national predisposition towards fixing, mending and adjusting things.

There aren't many countries where you can head to a local craftsperson with the knowledge that you'll find an artisan whose work may well match those of the most illustrious labels. And their services often come surprisingly cheap. Humble as they may be, these are respected jobs – shoemaking and mending was one of the few professions that had its own corporation (the ancestor of a trade union) in medieval Florence and its importance in Italian history remains appreciated.

Though the amount of specialised mending shops may have diminished, an increasing number of young apprentices are picking up the trade again. Many of these shops have been passed down through generations, and duties are carried out with a devoted, stubborn dedication to a job *fatto bene* – done well.

News kiosks: *Read all about it*

One outing that has long been a staple of many peoples' routine is a visit to the *edicola* to catch up on current events or grab a speciality magazine or newspaper of choice. Each of the nation's 15,000 newsstands is a mini monument to the power of print. The best-run operations offer both local and international publications and manage to pack in more than 500 titles from broadsheets to glossies in just a few square metres of display space.

In the summer, the kiosks are especially popular as Italians look to enjoy their leisure time by stacking up on a mix of gossip titles, sports and news dailies as well as weeklies and the demanding crossword puzzles from *La Settimana Enigmistica*. Customers are treated to particularly attentive service as kiosk owners put aside special inserts or supplements for their regular clients, go the extra mile to hand deliver a copy or track down a back issue. And when it comes to the weekend, the *edicola* becomes a place where customers linger and discuss the goings-on in the neighbourhood or indulge in a heated discussion on the latest political drama, making it an integral part of the community.

METRI QUADRATI DI SPAZIO INFINITO
METRI QUADRATI DI SPAZIO INFINITO
518
, QUESTA NON È LA FELTRINELLI
«PAPIER» MAGAZINE D'ILLUS-TRATIONS THÈME N°6 COUPE DU MONDE PAR DIMANCHE
delirious museum
come vedere il mondo
BRAND
ELEPHANT
ModernMatter
Mother
flow

Trade fairs:
Best in show

Italy is home to thousands of businesses both big and small, so it's no surprise that the country holds a number of influential tradeshows at which brands can show off their wares. Milan's strategic position in the country's industrial heartland makes it the perfect host for such events – Salone del Mobile, the world's biggest and agenda-setting furniture fair, takes over the city's streets every spring. And it really does take over: while the majority of deals take place in the vast purpose-built Rho Fiera complex, the accompanying Fuorisalone includes some 1,500 events, exhibitions and cocktail parties held everywhere from hidden courtyards in grand *palazzi* to abandoned warehouses.

The country seemingly has a fair for everything: Genoa holds Salone Nautico, the Med's biggest annual yachting event; Bologna is host to both the industry-leading Children's Book Fair and Cersaie, the ceramic tile and bathroom furnishings show; and while Milan more than looks after furniture design and womenswear, Florence is where men's fashion takes the lead with its Pitti franchise. Of course, trade shows happen all over the world, but Italian fairs have recognised the importance of a key ingredient so often missing from the line up – fun.

Salone
del Mobile.
Milano
09_14.04.2019
Circolare esterna
Shuttle Bus
Ingresso Stampa Porta Sud
Press entrance Gate South
Taxi collettivo
Share taxi
Reception
Reception
Reception
ATTENZIONE
ATTENTION

Chapter 9

The grand tour

For a country of its size, Italy offers a remarkable sense of variety. Whether we're talking about landscape, tradition, cuisine or dialect, each of the 20 regions has its own identity. Nowhere is this contrast and distinction more obvious than on the streets of the nation's cities: you can often locate yourself by looking at a street scene alone. Join us on a jaunt from north to south, taking in the waterways of Venice, the sandy beaches of Naples and the ruins of Rome. All aboard!

Region by region:
Meet the neighbours

To the untrained eye Italy may appear replete with country-wide character traits but in truth it's a very young nation with many diverging attributes. It wasn't until 1861 that the kingdoms that occupied the different corners of the peninsula – from the Habsburgs in the north to the Bourbons in the south, via the Papal State in the middle – were unified under the flag of the Savoys.

Centuries of invasion and occupation have brought myriad influences to this strategic land in the middle of the Mediterranean and each of its 20 regions has fostered its own distinct identity. Let's take a tour...

Valle d'Aosta

Population: 125,000
Size: 3,261 sq km
Regional capital: Aosta
Cuisine: Hearty food – chamois stew served with polenta, French-inspired cheeses and a grappa and coffee mix drunk from a multi-spouted *grolla*.
Local expression: *Fat pa dzeudzé l'arbro a la rutse.*
Translation: You shouldn't judge a tree by its bark.
Meaning: Don't judge according to appearances.
Famous landmark: Mont Blanc, the highest peak in Europe, tops out at nearly 5,000m.

Full of Alpine slopes and winter skiers, Valle d'Aosta sits on the borders of France and Switzerland. French is the second language in this autonomous and tiny region and Francophile influences pervade the cuisine, architecture and unique Valdôtain dialect.

Liguria

Population: 1.5 million
Size: 5,416 sq km
Regional capital: Genoa
Cuisine: The birthplace of basil pesto, originally produced to keep sailors safe from scurvy. Twisted *trofie* pasta, focaccia and seafood add to the shore's plentiful offerings.
Local expression: *Sciusciâ e sciorbî no se peu.*
Translation: You can't suck and blow at the same time.
Meaning: You can't do everything at once.
Famous landmark: Piazza de Ferrari, Genoa's main square, is renowned for the striking bronze fountain at its centre built in 1936.

A crescent of coast stretching from the South of France to Tuscany, and home to the Italian Riviera, Liguria is marked by steep mountains descending into much of its 350km of rocky seafront.

Piedmont

Population: 4.3 million
Size: 25,387 sq km
Regional capital: Turin
Cuisine: Raw and cooked meats, plus big red Barolos, truffles and gianduja chocolates.
Local expression: *Parla pa!*
Translation: Do not speak!
Meaning: Impressive!
Famous landmark: The Mole Antonelliana in Turin was initially designed in 1863 as a synagogue by architect Alessandro Antonelli. It now houses the Museo Nazionale del Cinema.

Sitting at the foot of the Alps, Piedmont's rolling landscape and capital city are famously elegant. It offers some of Italy's most refined cuisine and wine and is credited as the birthplace of the Slow Food movement.

Lombardy

Population: 10 million
Size: 23,844 sq km
Regional capital: Milan
Cuisine: Rice and polenta-based dishes as well as rich stews influenced by its Swiss neighbours.
Local expression: *Fa ballà l'oeugg.*
Translation: Make your eyes dance.
Meaning: Be careful, keep an eye out.
Famous landmark: The region's lakes, from Como and Iseo to Garda and Maggiore. Naturally formed at the end of the last ice age, they've been frequented since Roman times.

Running along the border of Switzerland, Lombardy is the country's richest region. Known as Italy's industrial heartland, it is home to the booming fashion and design sectors and its financial centre. It is also the top agricultural area.

Trentino-Alto Adige

Population: 1 million
Size: 13,606 sq km
Regional capital: Trento
Cuisine: Meat-rich alpine fare that represents its Austrian roots, from *spätzle* to *apfelküchel.*
Local expression: *Ama l'ert ma teite al pian.*
Translation: Love the heights, but keep on the plains.
Meaning: Have lofty ambitions but be realistic.
Famous landmark: A UNESCO World Heritage site, the Dolomites started as coral reefs beneath the Tethys Ocean 250 million years ago.

Italy's northernmost region links the two autonomous Alpine territories of Italian-speaking Trentino with German-speaking Alto Adige, annexed from the Austro-Hungarian empire in 1919. Both are known for their pristine nature, lakes and stunning mountains.

Emilia-Romagna

Population: 4.5 million
Size: 22,453 sq km
Regional capital: Bologna
Cuisine: Home of Italian classics such as Parmigiano-reggiano, balsamic vinegar and Prosciutto di Parma as well as fresh pasta.
Local expression: *Al premm turtel, an ven mai bel.*
Translation: The first tortellino never comes out well.
Meaning: First attempts are never successful.
Famous landmark: The city of Ravenna's gold mosaicked churches and mausolea reveal the region's domination in the Western Roman Empire, Ostrogoth and Byzantine periods.

Emilia-Romagna vaunts vast food production. It is also home to the country's zippiest car brands including Lamborghini, Ferrari, and Maserati plus the University of Bologna, the oldest in the world.

Veneto

Population: 5 million
Size: 18,407 sq km
Regional capital: Venice
Cuisine: Risotto and polenta precede pasta here; staples include *sarde in saor* and *baccalà mantecato.*
Local expression: *Averghe el morbin.*
Translation: To be agitated like a horse.
Meaning: Not being able to stay still.
Famous landmark: Piazza San Marco, begun in the 9th century and finished in the 19th, monumentalises Venice's many centuries of glory.

The northern Adriatic region was long the gateway between East and West thanks to seafaring Venice; today its bustling production of glass, jewellery, furniture and the world's best-selling bubbly, Prosecco, maintain its position as a wealthy international trading hub.

Friuli Venezia Giulia

Population: 1.2 million
Size: 7,847 sq km
Regional capital: Trieste
Cuisine: *Frico*, smoked trout and cherry dumplings reflect its Austro-Hungarian heritage.
Local expression: *Val plui un ucel in man che cent par ajar.*
Translation: A bird in your hand is worth more than a hundred in flight.
Meaning: What you have is more valuable than what you could have.
Famous landmark: The Viennese-style Piazza dell'Unità d'Italia overlooks the Gulf of Trieste.

A mix of a region at the borders of Slovenia and Austria, it includes Slavic, Germanic and Italian areas where the dialect of Friulano is spoken. It was contested ground during the First World War.

Tuscany

Population: 3.7 million
Size: 22,987 sq km
Regional capital: Florence
Cuisine: Rustic soups and legumes, Fiorentina T-bone steak and *pane sciocco,* bread made with very little salt that's served with the region's salame.
Local expression: *Boia dé!*
Translation: Assassin!
Meaning: Damn!
Famous landmark: Florence's Duomo has been the city's tallest building since 1436, when Brunelleschi's great dome was built to rival the Pantheon in Rome.

Tuscany's rolling hills have become the popular epitome of the Italian countryside. The cradle of the Renaissance, its art is equally iconic along with its medieval villages, rural villas and frescoed churches.

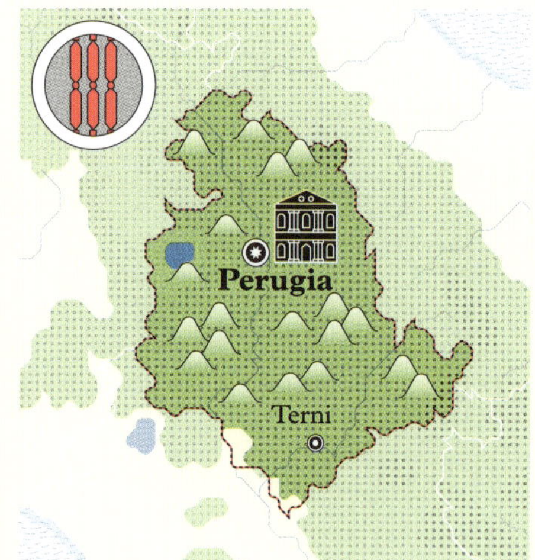

Umbria

Population: 900,000
Size: 8,464 sq km
Regional capital: Perugia
Cuisine: White and black truffles, pasta and local pork – served cured or in *porchetta.* The region also makes an esteemed peppery olive oil.
Local expression: *Co lu tempu e la paia maturaro nchì e nespule.*
Translation: Even medlar fruits ripen with time and hay.
Meaning: Be patient.
Famous landmark: The Basilica di San Francesco in the hillside town of Assisi is filled with early Renaissance masterpieces.

Italy's green heart, Umbria is spread over fertile valleys of vineyards and olive groves. The area is still dotted with monasteries from medieval times.

Marche

Population: 1.5 million
Size: 9,401 sq km
Regional capital: Ancona
Cuisine: Fried Ascolane olives stuffed with meat and cheese, *ciauscolo* spreadable sausage, and *vincisgrassi lasagne* with veal ragù.
Local expression: *Cala jo da sto ceregio.*
Translation: Get off the cherry tree.
Meaning: Don't be full of yourself.
Famous landmark: The UNESCO-listed 15th-century Palazzo Ducale in Urbino houses art by Piero della Francesca, Paolo Uccello and Raphael.

This hilly region in central Italy is set between the Apennines and the Adriatic coast, where winding roads lead down to a trainline that runs the entirety of its shore – roughly 170km. A region of makers, it's famed for its shoes, furniture and accordions.

Campania

Population: 5.8 million
Size: 13,671 sq km
Regional capital: Naples
Cuisine: Italy's capital of pizza (and locally made buffalo mozzarella) enjoys deep-fried everything, anchovies in all forms and lard-baked pastries.
Local expression: *Adda passà 'a nuttata.*
Translation: The night needs to pass.
Meaning: With patience, you will see through a difficult time.
Famous landmark: Capri's Grotta Azzurra (Blue Grotto) is a natural sea cave with crystalline waters that shimmer in iridescent shades of turquoise.

Mount Vesuvius dominates the landscape; the volcano wreaked havoc on ancient societies but provides rich agriculture. The Amalfi Coast with its postcard-perfect scenes needs no introduction.

Basilicata

Population: 600,000
Size: 10,073 sq km
Regional capital: Potenza
Cuisine: Altamura bread, *cavatelli* pasta, *soppressata* sausage spread and grilled horsemeat. Everything is seasoned with local Senise peppers.
Local expression: *Tèn' la facc' com' a r pret lesc.*
Translation: Having a face like a smooth stone.
Meaning: To have the nerve to do something.
Famous landmark: The caves of the Sassi of Matera; inhabited by humans since prehistoric times, they are now filled with shops and inns.

The instep of Italy's boot, Basilicata conserves the primordial look of its extensive mountains, forests and caves, where signs of what are thought to be the first settlements in Italy date back to 7000BC.

Puglia

Population: 4 million
Size: 19,541 sq km
Regional capital: Bari
Cuisine: Eggless *orecchiette* pasta served with chilli-flecked turnip tops as well as vegetable and fish-based dishes with copious olive oil.
Local expression: *Citt citt nmezz la chiazz.*
Translation: Silent silent in the middle of the square.
Meaning: Better not to spread gossip around.
Famous landmark: The perfectly octagonal Castel del Monte was built by emperor Frederick II in the 13th century. It was used as a hunting lodge, prison and refuge through the centuries.

Italy's 400km-long heel has more coastline than any other region. Largely flat and agricultural, Puglia produces 40 per cent of Italy's olive oil and is known for its conical white *trulli* huts.

Lazio

Population: 5.9 million
Size: 17,232 sq km
Regional capital: Rome
Cuisine: Belly-filling pasta dishes – *cacio e pepe*, carbonara, *amatriciana, gricia* – and offal.
Local expression: *Bonanotte ar secchio.*
Translation: Goodnight to the bucket.
Meaning: And that's that.
Famous landmark: The Colosseum – the arch-lined travertine monument was constructed from 72AD TO 80AD. It remains an icon of Rome and its flourishing ancient society.

Beyond its sandy Tyrrhenian coast, Lazio holds splendours of the past including Hadrian's Tivoli estate, Ostia Antica's remains and Tarquinia's Etruscan ruins, plus Rome's dense conglomeration of some of the world's most significant ancient sites.

Abruzzo

Population: 1.3 million
Size: 10,831 sq km
Regional capital: L'Aquila
Cuisine: Ventricina pork sausages, lamb skewers and fresh pasta cut *alla chitarra.* Abruzzo is also a producer of world-famous saffron.
Local expression: *Stè a mezz a na pezz' di casc'.*
Translation: To be in the middle of a bit of cheese.
Meaning: To be cosy and protected.
Famous landmark: Gran Sasso, the highest massif in the Apennine mountains.

Nearly half composed of nature reserves and parkland, Abruzzo's rugged landscape combines snow-topped peaks and pristine seashore. The region is also home to some of the last large fauna found in the country, including local species of wolves, bears and red deer.

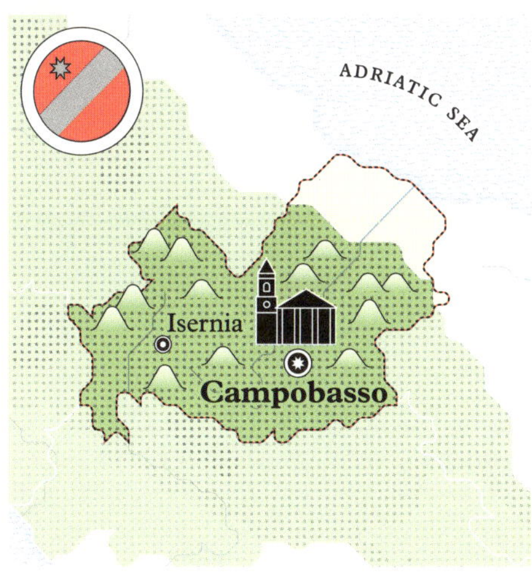

Molise

Population: 300,000
Size: 4,461 sq km
Regional capital: Campobasso
Cuisine: *Cavatelli* and fusilli pasta, plus *caciocavallo* cheese, fire-cooked *aracanato* cod and crusty-roasted *pampanella* pork strips.
Local expression: *Prèta che ròciola n'mmétte carpìa.*
Translation: A stone that rolls never makes moss.
Meaning: Someone who moves too frequently will never settle.
Famous landmark: The Norman Castello Monforte – a blocky, stone fortress that overlooks Campobasso from atop the Colle Sant'Antonio.

The pastoral, oft-forgotten 20th region was only created in 1970 when it split from Abruzzo. The area has a strong artisanal history: it produces church bells in Agnone and bagpipes in Scampoli.

Calabria

Population: 1.9 million
Size: 15,222 sq km
Regional capital: Catanzaro
Cuisine: Spicy, *peperoncino*-flavoured pasta dishes, many with ancient Greek roots. Sweet Tropea onions and bergamot citrus are unique to the area.
Local expression: *Zappare all'acqua.*
Translation: Hoeing into water.
Meaning: To do something useless.
Famous landmark: The Riace Bronzes – full-size male figures from Greece dating back to 450BC – were discovered on the Ionian seabed in 1972.

Italy's toe is one of the least tourist-explored regions in the country but it has made a name for itself thanks to the region's culinary exports of which *nduja* (a spicy spreadable sausage) is one of the most famous.

Sicily

Population: 5 million
Size: 25,832 sq km
Regional capital: Palermo
Cuisine: Sardines, swordfish and local catches, plus *arancine*, aubergine *caponata* and *cannoli.*
Local expression: *Cu nasci tunnu, un po' moriri piscispata.*
Translation: A tuna cannot die a swordfish.
Meaning: It's hard to change your characteristics.
Famous landmark: The Valley of the Temples in Agrigento with its Greek remains stands as a reminder of Sicily's multifaceted heritage.

Italy's largest region, Sicily is at the crossroads of the Mediterranean and was once a magnet for invaders – Greek, Roman, Arabic, Norman, French and Spanish – who all left their mark on the culture, architecture and cuisine of the island.

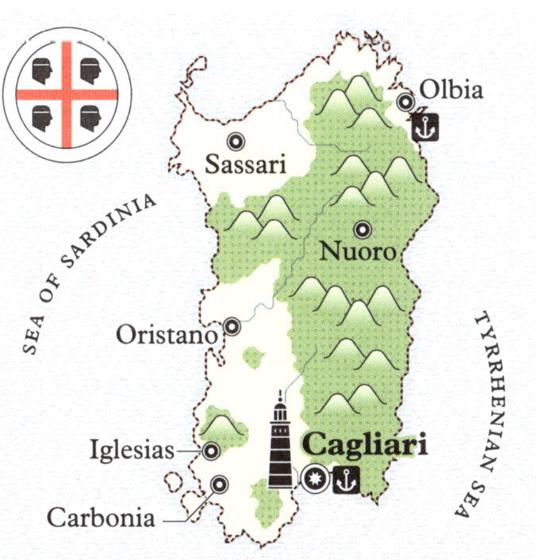

Sardinia

Population: 1.6 million
Size: 24,100 sq km
Regional capital: Cagliari
Cuisine: Fregola pasta, *bottarga* fish eggs and paper-thin *pane carasau*, plus sheep's milk ricotta.
Local expression: *E mera è cosa.*
Translation: A lot is something.
Meaning: Be content with what you have.
Famous landmark: Basilica di Nostra Signora in Cagliari draws crowds eager to visit the church's storied statue of the Virgin Mary.

The prehistoric Nuragic people settled in Sardinia and represent one of Europe's oldest civilizations. The island's northern coast is home to the resorts of Costa Smeralda, while there are swathes of unspoilt wilderness inland. With a strong regional identity, some have previously called for independence.

Population: 110,000
Known for: Its mountain athletes, from skier Gustav Thöni to mountaineer Tamara Lunger
Speciality dish: *Knödel*

Bolzano.

This is a place where the summers are hot and the winters are cold, the languages are many and the customs strange. Here, the roads are clean, the mountains tall and the sun is (almost) always shining. On the streets of Bolzano – or Bozen, or Balsan, depending on who you're talking to – climbing boots are as common as high heels (you never know when you might need to scale a mountain).

This tiny city in the country's northernmost corner stitches together the cultures that have shaped its history – South Tyrol was formerly part of the Austrian Empire, only ceded to Italy in 1919 – and its past is vibrantly evident in its architecture, food and languages (of which there are three, officially: German, Italian and Ladin).

Here, the fresh mountain air is sweet with the smell of apple strudel, and establishments serve up *Knödel* (dumplings made with bread, eggs, onion and herbs), Alpine spritzes – complete with a dash of fragrant elderflower syrup – and quick short shots of grappa. Influenced by both sides of the border, residents greet you with "Hoi" and "Ciao" while typical Tyrolean architecture lines the city's *piazze* which fill with stalls for the daily *mercato*.

The best place to see the city, though, is from the mountains – once you get up high you can see everything: the cathedral-like warehouses, the thick roofs and narrow paths of the old town, skinny houses and sprawling villas, contemporary architecture, museums and spires. And the three rivers, Eisack, Etsch and Talfer, that criss-cross through it all are a reminder that nature is never too far away. The ever-present peaks, lakes and forests of the Dolomites are there to explore for a hike, a ski or swim.

Bolzano provides excitement and fun, laziness and idleness. It is an ancient and proud city, but it thinks in a contemporary way and on its own terms. At once both a small town and the closest thing to a buzzing metropolis in South Tyrol, Bolzano has struck that hard-to-find balance between innovation and tradition, hard work and leisure.

About the writers: The co-founders of communication bureau franzLAB, Kunigunde Weissenegger & Anna Quinz live in Bolzano and are driven by a curiosity for the beautiful, positive and contemporary.

1

1.
Rino Vullo (or Cobo to his friends) is the owner of aperitivo spot Fischbänke

2.
Known as "The Gateway to the Dolomites", Bolzano is surrounded by mountains. The Ritten/Renon cable car takes you to the highest plateau for far-reaching views and multiple hikes; there are more than 170 trails in the area

2

1

2

3

4

5

6

7

1.
The city's proximity to the outdoors is a big draw for its canine residents
2.
Piazza Walther, or Der Waltherplatz, takes its name from the central monument of medieval poet and bard Walther von der Vogelweide
3.
Castel Mareccio dates back to the 13th century – its oldest tower was built by the noble Maretsch family
4.
Much like the rest of Italy, locals like to indulge in an *aperitivo lungo*
5.
The Alpine spritz – or Hugo – is a mix of elderflower syrup, mint and prosecco and was invented in South Tyrol
6.
The 100-room Laurin hotel was opened in 1910 by Franz Staffler and is still run by his descendents
7.
An expressive door handle at the Mercantile Museum of Bolzano
8.
Via Dr Joseph Streiter was named after a former mayor of the city and is lined with historic architecture
9.
The new home of Museion – the Museum of Modern and Contemporary Art – was designed by Berlin architects Krüger Schuberth Vandreike in 2008
10.
A resident takes a brisk stroll
11.
Markets – such as this one on Piazza delle Erbe/Obstmarkt – are an important part of life in Bolzano
12.
Parfumerie Ferrari was founded in 1952

8

9

10

11

12

Population: 200,000
Known for: Coffee – the city's free port, established in 1719, transformed Trieste into Italy's coffee trade-capital. Now, residents drink twice as much as the rest of the nation
Speciality dish: *Prosciutto cotto in crosta*

Trieste.

I think I had always known that Trieste was a little different, but it never truly sank in until the early 1990s when I leafed through an old atlas. I noticed that the bathyscaphe – a deep-sea submersible – that first shed light on the Mariana Trench was named after my hometown. "Why Trieste?" I pondered.

That question sparked an ongoing hunt for the answer, which I later discovered was linked to the Austrian Empire's decision to establish their free port here, turning the trading outpost into one of the 18th-century's most attractive cities – and ultimately the place where the underwater research vessel was built. I dream of travelling back in time to see the city in its neoclassical glory days.

Sandwiched between the Alps and the Adriatic, Trieste sits at a European crossroads where Latin, Slavic and German influences combine. My Istrian grandmother would cook Hungarian goulash, cumin-seed-flavoured sauerkraut and fish swimming in tomato, garlic and parsley; at dinner, we spoke the same Triestine dialect that James Joyce loved.

I often feel like I'm swinging between the past and the present – a feeling the writer Jan Morris perfectly described in her book *Trieste and the Meaning of Nowhere*. It's a common sensation here: "Sometimes we forget our blood is well mixed," a local songwriter once told me. For people from former Yugoslavia, I live in the western gateway but, according to my German friends, I belong to the south. To other Italians, I may live in the Balkans – out on the eastern frontier. No wonder Trieste's identity is hard to pin down.

The bora – the strong northeasterly wind which buffets the Adriatic – is my antidote to procrastination. When it is particularly restless, I take refuge in one of the city's historic coffee shops and think about the people who shaped the city. Nobel-prize winner Abdus Salam founded the International Centre for Theoretical Physics here and Ottavio Missoni chose the city for his first workshop after escaping Croatia at the end of the Second World War. But why Trieste? I finally got my answer in 2014 when I decided to walk all the way from London, where I lived at the time, back to my hometown. I chose to stay.

About the writer: Head of *TriestePrima* newsroom, the city's most followed website, Nicolò Giraldi has published many books about Trieste.

1.
Francesco Rossetti Cosulich is the president of Trieste's Yacht Club Adriaco, founded in 1903
2.
Located at the end of the Canal Grande, Sant'Antonio Taumaturgo is the city's largest Catholic church

1

2

1

SALATRIPCOVICH
2

TRIESTE - ITALIA
0233
90
3

4

IL PICCOLO
IL PICCOLO
5

6

7

8

9

10

11

12

13

1.
The Hotel Riviera & Maximilian's lido in nearby Grignano

2.
Built in 1936 as a bus station, Sala Tripcovich was converted into a theatre in the 1990s

3.
Arabica beans at Illy's warehouse; roughly 2.5m 60kg bags pass through the city annually

4.
Trieste has its own coffee lexicon: here an espresso is known as *un nero*

5.
The *edicola* on Via Cesare Battisti

6.
Piazza dell'Unità d'Italia and Trieste City Hall's grand architecture harks back to the city's status as the most important port of Mitteleuropa

7.
Post-dip at the Pedocin sea-bathing station – the only one in Europe where the sexes are still segregated

8.
Trieste's population is one of Italy's oldest with an average age of 48.4 years, but younger *triestini* are making their mark

9.
Ursus, the 75m-high crane which towers above the port, is one of the city's most famous landmarks

10.
Trieste faces due west, giving the city long, golden summer days

11.
Time for a Maxibon

12.
Trieste's quays, avenues and alleyways are littered with ghosts of the past

13.
The city may be filled with a plethora of central European surnames but its people are still positively bronzed

Population: 1.39 million
Known for: Fashion and design – Milan is home to exclusive shopping street Via Montenapoleone and Salone del Mobile, the world's largest furniture fair
Speciality dish: *Risotto alla Milanese*

Milan.

Milan is not an easy city to love. While Venice and Rome grab your attention with their lavish architectural attributes, with Milan you need to be patient. It takes time to understand its beauty but once you do the rewards are many.

My first impressions of Milan came from a striking spread in an issue of *National Geographic* from the early 1990s. It captured the Lombard capital in all its nuanced shades of grey: a gritty cityscape punctuated by stately buildings, traffic and, of course, runway shows with leggy supermodels. At university in California, I saw the postwar Milan of Italy's economic miracle up on the big screen in Antonioni's *La Notte* and Visconti's *Rocco e i Suoi Fratelli.* Soon after, I too joined the band of migrants like the fictional Rocco and set down roots in this uniquely Italian metropolis that attracts inquisitive and industrious types from near and far.

This cosmopolitan component of Milan is what makes the city so vibrant. It is one of those magical ingredients so often overlooked when sizing up cities. We locals benefit from creatives who decamp here with their talents in tow and open new ventures in everything from fashion and food to design and media.

Of course Milan has a few signature landmarks – I'll never tire of the splendour of the Duomo or Gio Ponti's cigarette-slim Pirelli skyscraper – but the city's charm is generally a more subtle affair. Entryways in residential *palazzi* offer a treasure trove of design details: fanciful floor patterns in beautiful stone, standout light fixtures, gorgeous wood panelling. Look up and you'll be treated to a world in bloom as flowers and plants cascade from balconies and rooftops. The most interesting locales are often secreted away in hidden courtyards behind an unassuming façade.

People like to say somewhat pejoratively that Milan is where Italy gets down to business. It's a workaholic city. Yet there's a sense of possibility and promise not found elsewhere. Milan is an Italian city but it's a European city too. That is to say it's a dynamic city with an eye on the future, not on the past.

About the writer: A native of California, Ivan Carvalho has been based in Italy since 2003. He has worked as MONOCLE'S Milan correspondent since 2007.

1

2

1.
Milan is home to *Corriere della Sera*, one of Italy's leading daily newspapers. This *edicola* near its offices is run by Fabrizio Prestinari and is arguably the city's best
2.
Leafy apartments in Brera, one of Milan's most enchanting and sought-after neighbourhoods

10
12

1

2

3

4

5

6

1.
Milanese *portinai* – doormen and doorwomen – are known for their friendly nature

2.
The 60m-high Torre building was designed by Dutch architecture firm OMA and is the latest addition to the Fondazione Prada

3.
The Arco della Pace on the edge of Parco Sempione was designed in 1807 by architect Luigi Cagnola

4.
As one of Europe's most polluted cities Milan is working hard to reduce car use and has introduced ambitious plans for new cycle schemes

5.
Maurizio Stocchetto is the owner of Bar Basso, the after-party venue of choice during Salone del Mobile

6.
Many of Milan's rooftop spaces are home to pocket-sized floral oases

7.
The Milanese may be habitually in a hurry but when it comes to drinking and dining they know how to slow things down a notch

8.
A staple of the city's cuisine, *risotto alla Milanese* is imbued with saffron

9.
Fondazione Prada is the country's leading contemporary art venue

10.
Sky-high statues atop the gothic Duomo di Milano. With some 3,400 sculptures in total, there are more figures on this cathedral than any other building in the world

11.
A green-framed balcony on Via Zecca Vecchia

12.
Housed in a former railway station, La Balera dell'Ortica is a *trattoria* and classic Italian dancing hall

13.
Construction on the Duomo began in 1386 but it wasn't completed for another six centuries

7

8

9

10

11

12

13

Population: 50,000
Known for: Its watery location – the city is situated on a collection of 118 small islands connected by more than 400 bridges
Speciality dish: *Cichèti*

Venice.

I was seven years old when my father received a job offer in Mestre – the town on *terraferma* across the bridge from Venice. It was soon decided that he could endure a short commute to enable us to live in the city that most only dream of inhabiting. We stayed for three years.

Contrary to what most people think, life in Venice is as easy as it is beautiful – and for a child it is simply magical. I was allowed to explore on my own and spent evenings playing football and hide-and-seek in the city's hidden *campi* (squares), inhaling the briny air. Some days would start with the wail of the sirens that signal the arrival of *acqua alta* (high water) – an unorthodox alarm clock that could mean a day off from school. Venice is a dreamlike labyrinth of pink *calli* (narrow streets) criss-crossed with bridges and canals. The city offers itself without restraint to anyone willing to explore it.

The hordes of tourists can sometimes make it feel like a theme park but they blindly stick to the same routes, so it is easy for locals (and adventurers) to get around and feel they have access to the *real* Venice. Slip down some of the quieter canals in Cannaregio and you might spot parents picking their children up from nursery or walking the dog: snapshots that remind you that this is a living, working city.

In *Watermark*, one of the most vivid odes to the city ever written, Joseph Brodsky claims that water is like time and provides beauty with its double. He's right. In Venice – where water is everywhere you look – time itself is more beautiful. Just observe the way the warm light finds its way around the pastel-tinted *palazzi* and glimmers amber through your spritz glass; sit on a bench in Sant'Elena listening to the kids play under the pines and watch the cats slowly slinking towards the Biennale pavilions; or venture out late at night, when the lampposts guide you through the mist that floods the silent, deserted *calli*. It's in these moments that you feel time as a physical presence. Not threatening, not melancholic, not racing but time as human and real as it can get – and it fills Venice with wonder.

About the writer: Like any writer worth their salt, Beatrice Carmi has a cat named after a literary figure – Huysmans.

1

2

1.
Venice is car-free – as such it boasts perhaps the most glamorous taxi fleet of any city in the world

2.
The Basilica di Santa Maria della Salute was the result of a promise: after a devastating plague ravaged the city in 1630, the Venetians appealed to the Madonna, pledging to build a church in her honour in exchange for salvation

1

2

3

4

5

6

1.
The saltwater lagoon surrounding the city is home to more than 50 islands including colourful Burano

2.
As the gateway for coffee into Europe in the 17th century, Venice still takes its caffeine very seriously

3.
Murano – another island in the lagoon – is famous for its glass

4.
Navigating the city's warren of alleyways can be tricky but 4,000 black stencilled street signs – known as *nizioleti* – aid the process

5.
Agostino Amadi's boatyard is one of the last of its kind on Burano

6.
Napoleon allegedly called Piazza San Marco "the drawing room of Europe"

7.
There are roughly 400 licensed gondoliers in the city

8.
Vaporetti are the area's water-buses; ACTV stations or *fermate* act as floating stops for the network

9.
A Venetian street-sign-painter

10.
Each gondola is made of up to eight different types of wood

11.
A policeman on jet-ski patrol

12.
Venice's iconic *bàcari* (backstreet bars) dispence *cichèti (*small savoury snacks) washed down with a spritz

7

8

9

10

11

12

Population: 870,000
Known for: Juventus – the most decorated football club in Italian history, it is the only team in the world to have won all official international cups and championships
Speciality dish: *Vitello tonnato*

Turin.

According to the national stereotype the Turinese are polite to the point of annoyance – they'll never tell you what they really want or mean. And there's some truth to it: they, like their city, are often forcefully modest, subdued and reserved.

The former Italian capital – and previous base for the now-exiled royal Savoy family – features all the symbols of pomp you'd expect from a monarchic seat: regal palaces, hunting lodges and plenty of statues of warriors on horseback. But for the most part, Turin presents an orderly face of prim white-fronted *palazzi*. Ambling under its porticoes (built so that the king could attend mass without getting his feet wet), the city feels more European than Italian – perhaps a whiff of French air escaping through the cracks between the peaks of the nearby Alps.

For all its elegance, Turin was long thought of as the grey car capital of the country – nothing but the final "T" in the acronym Fiat (Fabbrica Italiana Automobili Torino) and a cold northern city where citizens of the south would begrudgingly relocate so they could work at the factory. But spend enough time in the city's restaurants and bars and you'll realise Turin is warm and red-blooded – red like the meat that cooks in our juicy *brasato* or red like the thick Barbera and Barolo wines produced in the hills.

Born as a Roman encampment, Turin inherited a pleasingly perpendicular grid of streets. Learning to drive my Piaggio scooter as a teenager, I felt reassured: it's hard to get lost here. Unless, of course, you want to – then you should take the windy roads up into the hills that flank the city. Seen from up high, Turin feels peaceful, lying low under the embrace of the mountains that tower proudly in the background.

A cohort of young Turinese creatives has modernised the city: they have made this a place to dance until dawn at raucous riverside bars, started bands and founded graphic design studios. But behind this innovative streak, there's an old-fashioned patina to everyday life. Turin still has the air of a bourgeois, 19th century drawing-room – but it will never show off about it.

About the writer: Chiara Rimella is MONOCLE's Culture editor. Having grown up in Turin she later moved to London, but is always keen to return to her family home and get the Piaggio engine revving.

1.
A classic Fiat on Piazza Vittorio Veneto; the city is the birthplace of the car manufacturer
2.
At 167.5m tall, Mole Antonelliana towers above Turin – it is also featured on the Italian two cent coin

1

2

1

2

3

4

5

6

7

8

9

1.
The rooftop test track at Fiat's Lingotto factory, designed by engineer Giacomo Mattè-Trucco

2.
The prim Galleria Subalpina was designed by Pietro Carrera and is home to the city's beloved Cinema Romano

3.
The *bicerin* – an espresso laced with melted chocolate and cream – is a long-standing Turinese favourite

4.
Rowers at the Parco del Valentino

5.
Gianduja chocolate – which contains roughly 30 per cent hazelnut paste – at Guido Gobino is cut to size from 3kg triangular bars; the Turinese were the first to make chocolate in solid form

6.
The *portici*, or arcades, at Piazza San Carlo; this area is home to San Carlo dal 1973 and Olympic, two of the city's most luxurious retailers

7.
Gigi Raiola runs Libreria Luxemburg – the oldest bookshop in the city

8.
Caffè Torino opened in Piazza San Carlo in 1903

9.
The city centre is a mix of architectural styles from art nouveau to baroque

10.
The Vittorio Emanuele I bridge over the Po, Italy's longest river

11.
All public drinking fountains in the city – known as *torèt* – feature a bull, the city's emblem

12.
Private gardens and courtyards often await behind grandiose doorways

13.
This café was named after the bronze statue of Emanuele Filiberto in Piazza San Carlo

14.
Raising a glass at Caffè Mulassano – supposedly the birthplace of *tramezzini* (Italy's answer to triangular finger sandwiches)

11

10

12

13

14

Population: 2.83 million
Known for: Its storied past – according to legend the city was officially founded in 753BC but evidence suggests that the area was inhabited long before that
Speciality dish: *Pasta carbonara*

Rome.

The seat of the unified Italian state is sometimes called the "Third Rome" by historians: first came ancient Rome, then Rome as centre of the Catholic church, and finally Rome as capital. But why the history lesson you might ask? Well, history is *everything* in Rome. Here, it is impossible to ignore the passing of time: the city's past is written in its architecture, food and even the way its residents talk. Yes, there are daily inefficiencies that can provoke hair tearing, but it is also a city whose blissful intransigence is its very essence.

People often talk of layers of history, making comparisons to lasagne (incidentally a dish seldom served here) but the city's story is not easily categorised; there are no full stops or parentheses that neatly frame its annals. Tradition seems to continuously trickle like the thousands of fountains that dot the *piazze*: a familiar grey habit darting out of sight behind the rusticated blocks of a baroque *palazzo* (nuns appear like street furniture and glimpsing them doing the most mundane of things becomes an urban activity), a pampered poodle frantically lapping at a water spout, the constant whining of the carpenter's bandsaw leaking from a scruffy workshop. And then the talking – so much talking everywhere.

It is also hard to describe the quintessential Roman but if it is possible to be gruff and haughty at the same time, you're getting close. Despite – or perhaps because of – the Vatican's presence, Romans tend to swear like troopers. Expletives and blasphemes punctuate the local *romanaccio* dialect (although the presence of a nun does tend to clean the language up somewhat).

Rome is at once provincial and cosmopolitan and its cuisine reflects this split personality. Astonishingly simple food dominates: artichokes are announced with much fanfare and sparse dressing, they simply have to be in season – and local.

Roughness and rectitude, raucousness and refinement, the city's mannerisms are rarely unpalatable. Who can bemoan the woeful infrastructure and lamentable city government when the way of doing things and the urban backdrop are so undeniably and infinitely agreeable?

About the writer: Identifying as "Anglo-Sardinian", David Plaisant is MONOCLE'S Rome correspondent. Born in Italy, he resettled in the capital in 2016 where he now covers everything from design to media.

1

2

1.
Papal Swiss Guards at the Vatican. In order to join the ranks candidates must be a Swiss citizen, Roman Catholic, aged between 19 and 30, at least 1.74m tall, unwed and willing to serve 26 months or more

2.
Piazza Navona inherited its oval shape from the ancient perimeter of the Stadium of Domitian. It now houses three baroque fountains – one of which was designed by Bernini

1

2

3

1.
Romantic Rome
2.
The Roman Forum is a bewildering collection of ruins whose hyper-urban setting is unmatched
3.
Palazzo Zuccari – also known as 'Monster House' – was designed by Federico Zuccari in 1590
4.
The classic 1969 Fiat 500
5.
A waiter at Gelateria Giolitti, the city's oldest ice cream parlour
6.
Rome's traffic jams are legendary
7.
Clothes shop Camiceria Mattioli on Via della Stelletta
8.
Furniture restorer Francesca Loffredi in her workshop, Gianfranco Squillace Restauratore
9.
Streetside blooms
10.
The Stadio Olimpico del Nuoto; built by the fascists in the 1930s, it was finished in 1959 by architects Enrico Del Debbio and Annibale Vitellozzi in anticipation of the 1960 Olympics
11.
Eating alfresco is a pleasure that's enjoyed in Rome as soon as the season allows
12.
Carciofi alla giudia (artichokes Jewish style) at Piperno restaurant
13.
Members ready for a spot of tennis at the Ministry of Foreign Affairs Club
14.
The Quartiere Coppedè in the upmarket Trieste neighbourhood is Rome's most opulent exponent of Liberty style – the Italian variant of art nouveau

4

5

6

7

8

9

10

11

12

13

14

Population: 960,000
Known for: Men's tailoring – the city's artisans have been crafting world-class shirts and suits since the 14th century
Speciality dish: *Pizza Napoletana*

Naples.

"Only Neapolitans are crazy enough to live next to an active volcano," a local told me as we sped along the seafront on his moped, sans helmets. The omnipresent Mount Vesuvius looms large at the water's edge – a symbol of this city's vibrant relationship with the ephemerality and intensity of life.

Baroque but battered, Naples captivates as much with its excessive beauty as with the scruffy, endearing charm of its streets. Here everything from the reckless driving culture, the balcony baskets lowered to collect groceries, the impenetrable Neapolitan dialect and the nighttime's spectral, sulphur-coloured lights points to an unmistakably singular culture born of ancient Greek, Spanish and French rule – and shaped by these people audacious enough to live in the shadow of a volcano.

The city that popularised opera knows no shortage of drama. Raffish, thrilling and glittering through the grime, Naples in recent years has written itself a happy plot twist – crime is down, the streets are cleaner, young people are launching hopeful new ventures and art and design denizens are moving in to set up shop. In the days of the Grand Tour, Naples was as essential a stop as Rome and now visitors are again being seduced by the dense history, southern beauty and head-spinning energy of the town, no longer hurrying straight off to Capri or the Amalfi Coast.

Years ago on my first visit to Naples, I sat down in a streetside restaurant in the Quartieri Spagnoli, a gritty, wonderful neighbourhood filled with murals of city heroes like Maradona and Totò, where strings of Christmas lights hang like garlands year-round over the narrow lanes. A local couple at the next table, noticing I was a novice, began passing over forkfuls of their various dishes. "Try this," they said. "You've never had anything this good," they said. I was unaccustomed to eating strangers' food in restaurants, but I was in a foreign country – the alien country of Naples – and amid the invigorating chaos, the surprising generosity of strangers and the mouthfuls of goodness, I was enchanted for life.

About the writer: Laura Rysman is MONOCLE's Florence-based Central Italy correspondent. She covers fashion, design, travel and art.

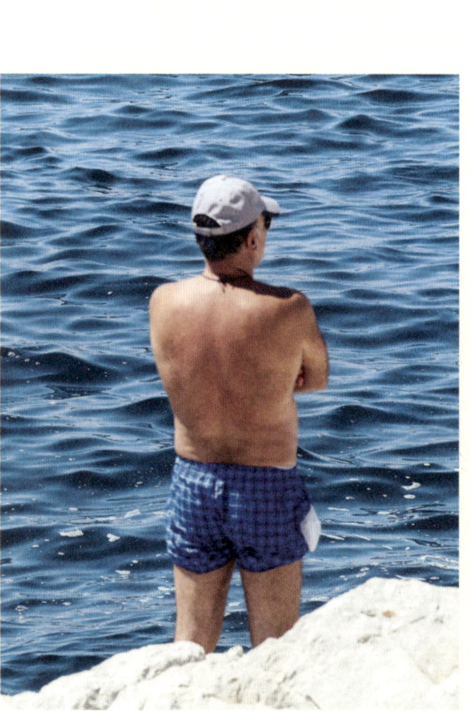

1

2

1.
In Naples everything faces the sea
2.
The city is a collage of baroque architecture, art nouveau-inspired villas and brutish concrete housing blocks all tumbling towards the coast

1

2

3

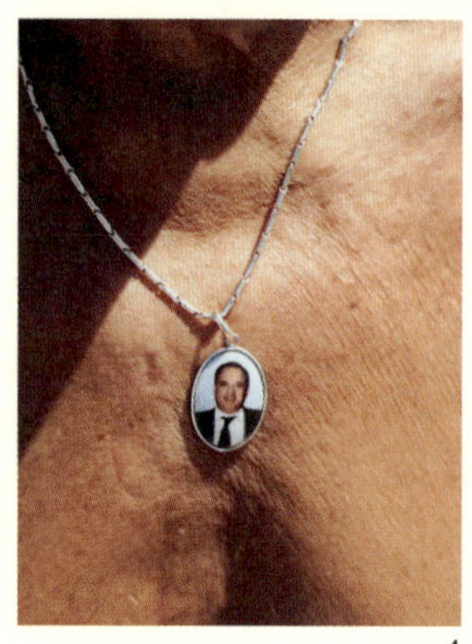

4

5

6

7

8

1.
The omnipresent Vesuvius is still active – it last erupted in March 1944

2.
Tie-maker Patrizio Cappelli looking sharp. The city has a strong sartorial identity and Naples is home to some of the world's most expensive suits

3.
A sunbather at Lido Marechiaro

4.
Lucky charm

5.
Gelato in Naples is supposedly richer and creamier than in the north of Italy

6.
Poker face

7.
Palazzo Panorama, a 1948 apartment tower in Vomero

8.
There are many markets in Naples; they sell everything from fresh produce and street food to clothing and second-hand furniture

9.
The Galleria Umberto I shopping arcade was completed in 1891 and features a glass domed roof and inlaid marble floor

10.
Striking a pose

11.
The undisputed birthplace of the doughy delight; there are more than 800 pizzerias in Naples today

12.
A sunny smile during *Ferragosto*, the public holiday in the middle of August that sees all of Italy head to the beach

13.
The historic Gran Caffè Gambrinus serves blends from Neopolitan roastery Caffè Moreno

14.
Naples's Centro Direzionale business district was designed by Japanese architect Kenzo Tange in 1982

9

10

11

12

13

14

Population: 660,000
Known for: Its markets – offering everything from farm produce to fashion, Palermo's famed *mercati alimentari* reflect the city's multicultural roots
Speciality dish: *Arancine*

Palermo.

Growing up as a child in Palermo, I was convinced the city was inland. I was aware of Mondello beach, where the nanny would take us on hot afternoons in the holidays and I would glance at the cruise ships peeking over the port gates, petrified by their monstrous scale. But all I could see at the end of the long streets cutting through the city were enormous mountains.

The sea was there but simultaneously it was not; and yet that never puzzled me. So many things that verge on absurdity make perfect sense in Palermo. On All Souls Day – crudely known in the city as "I Morti" (The Dead) – kids wake up to pastel-coloured sugar figurines, kindly gifted by dead relatives. I would eat them thinking about my grandfathers raising from their graves overnight.

Sugar and desserts are inextricably linked to the visual identity of the city. True happiness can be found elegantly wrapped in golden paper at Pasticceria Costa in the form of a watermelon pudding decorated with jasmine flowers. Pasticceria Oscar lures you in with an aggressively 1980s energy that translates into its sweet treats while the retro logo of Fratelli Magrì speaks of pure ricotta and marzipan. Picking desserts for Sunday lunch was nothing short of a ritual.

On the way back from school my friends and I would run to the botanical wonders of Villa Trabia – although I was never brave enough to climb to the top of the majestic ficus trees like the older kids did. Back then, I was unaware that the trees had been imported from Australia in the 19th century. The city often reveals itself through the presence of distant lands and memories of past civilizations can be found everywhere you look: Catholic churches decorated with byzantine mosaics, Arab palaces near avenues named after Spanish viceroys. In my imagination Palermo had also been a Chinese colony, as indicated by the pagoda-style Palazzina Cinese – in fact, just a royal residence from the Bourbon era.

Teenagers on scooters drive past it on their way to Mondello, ready to flock around the green ice cream shack on Piazza Valdesi. Sitting there on a warm day, tucking into a gelato brioche, it almost feels like being in any ordinary seaside town. Almost.

About the writer: London-based fashion designer Margherita Mazzola was born in Palermo. She's never lost her taste for the Sicilian city – or its treats.

1

2

1.
The Sicilian treat of granita is a smooth yet crunchy iced dessert, available in different flavours across the island
2.
Palermo is a melting pot: countless cultures from the Phoenicians and Greeks to the Spanish, French and Americans have all influenced the city

MI.FA. di GULLO LANA - COTONE - RICAMI - MERLETTI - TESSUTI NEONATO - FODERAMI - MERCERIE
COTONE - RICAMI - MERLETTI - TESSUTI NEONATO - FODERAMI - MERCERIE

1

2

3

4

5

6

7

8

9

1.
Palermo sits in a natural bowl surrounded by a ring of rocky hills and faces east across the Tyrrhenian Sea towards mainland Italy
2.
The beach at Mondello has crystal clear waters and scoops of old Italian charm
3.
Majorettes perform at a parade in the city centre
4.
Rudimentary Ape trucks line the streets by Mondello, selling everything from granita to fresh seafood
5.
A stone's throw from central Piazza Pretoria, La Stanza di Carta is a bookshop that stocks thousands of titles, from vintage books to contemporary releases
6.
Youths leap from the pier at Mondello
7.
A rare moment of peace
8.
Banco di Sicilia in the city's centre
9.
After the Second World War, the Old City's population shrank from 200,000 to 50,000 in 1974, with much of its architecture left to crumble
10.
The trickle of pioneering young Palermitans back into the city is a sign that the Sicilian capital is putting the darker decades of the second half of the 20th century behind it
11.
The former Libreria Dante has been home to Bisso Bistrot since 2014
12.
Via Roma runs through the city centre and is lined with 19th-century *palazzi*
13.
Palermo is famous for its sweet treats, from ricotta-stuffed *cannoli* to *cassata* (sponge cake layered with ricotta cheese and candied fruit)

10

11

12

13

The Monocle Book of ITALY

Acknowledgements

The Monocle Book of Italy
EDITORS
Chiara Rimella
Joe Pickard

DESIGNERS
Richard Spencer Powell
Giulia Tugnoli
Maria Hamer

PHOTO EDITORS
Matthew Beaman
Shin Miura
Lucy Pullicino

PRODUCTION
Jacqueline Deacon

Special thanks:
Stefano Dughera
Rebecca Ricci
Amy Richardson

Researchers:
Melkon Charchoglyan
Gabriele Dellisanti
Julia Webster Ayuso

Monocle
EDITORIAL DIRECTOR & CHAIRMAN
Tyler Brûlé

EDITOR IN CHIEF
Andrew Tuck

CREATIVE DIRECTOR
Richard Spencer Powell

BOOKS EDITOR
Joe Pickard

DEPUTY EDITOR
Molly Price

ASSISTANT EDITOR
Hester Underhill

DESIGNERS
Sam Brogan
Maria Hamer
Giulia Tugnoli

PHOTO EDITORS
Matthew Beaman
Shin Miura
Lucy Pullicino

PRODUCTION
Jacqueline Deacon

Writers:
Tyler Brûlé
Beatrice Carmi
Ivan Carvalho
Francesco Franchi
Nicolò Giraldi
Margherita Mazzola
Joe Pickard
David Plaisant
Molly Price
Anna Quinz
Chiara Rimella
Laura Rysman
Hester Underhill
Kunigunde Weissenegger

Photographers:
Mattia Balsamini
Finn Beales
Felix Brüggemann
Victoria Cagol
Gaia Cambiaggi
Guido Castagnoli
Elisabetta Claudio
Federico Covre
Ana Cuba
Claudia Ferri
Luigi Fiano
Christian Flatscher
Gianfranco Gallucci
Daniel Gebhart de Koekkoek
Bea De Giacomo
Stefan Giftthaler
Chiara Goia
Luca Grottoli
Mariano Herrera
Salva López
Sara Magni
Alex Majoli / Magnum Photos
Leonardo Magrelli
Luca Meneghel
Aliocha Merker
Domingo Milella
Shin Miura
James Mollison
Claudio Morelli
Piotr Niepsuj
Felix Odell
Stefan Olah
Martin Parr / Magnum Photos
Filippo Poni
Andrea Pugiotto
Rocco Rorandelli
Danilio Scarpati
Jens Schwarz
Jerome Sessini / Magnum Photos
Francesca Volpi
Eirini Vourloumis
Trisha Ward
Lukas Wassmann
Dan Wilton
Andrea Wyner

Images:
Alamy
Gallery Stock
Getty Images
Werner Huthmacher
Moreno Maggi
Shutterstock
View pictures

Illustrators:
Massimiliano Aurelio
Karin Kellner
Matteo Riva
Xihanation

Index

Index

About Monocle:
Magazine and more

In 2007, MONOCLE was launched as a monthly magazine briefing on global affairs, business, design and more. Today we have a thriving print business, a radio station, shops, cafés, books, films and events. At our core is the simple belief that there will always be a place for a brand that is committed to telling fresh stories, delivering good journalism and being on the ground around the world.

We're Zürich and London-based and have bureaux in Hong Kong, Tokyo, Los Angeles and Toronto. Over the years our editors and correspondents have come to understand what makes a nation tick. This knowledge is unpacked in this book and throughout our reporting on Monocle 24, in film at *monocle.com* and, of course, across our print and digital products.

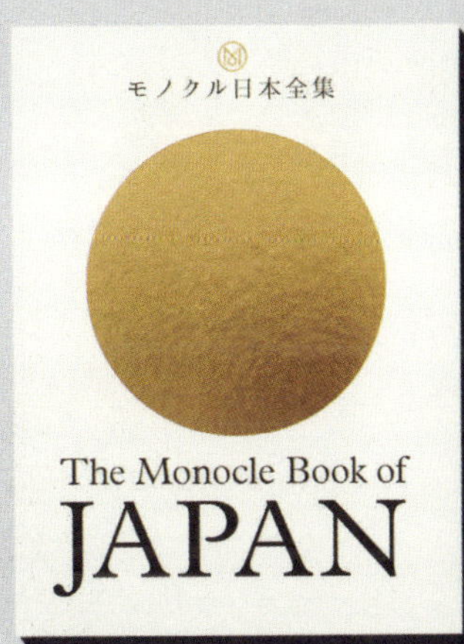

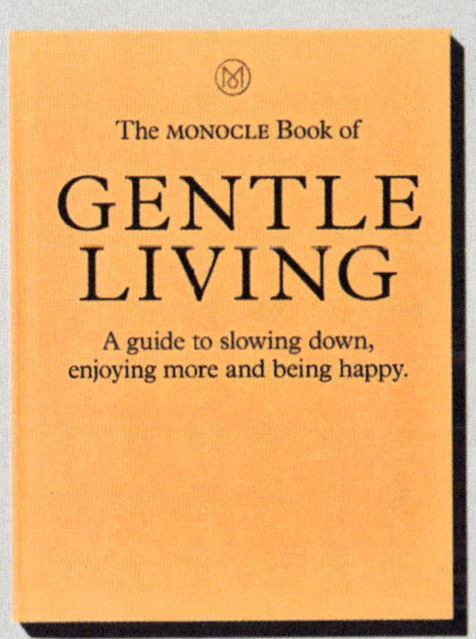

Monocle magazine

MONOCLE magazine is published 10 times a year, including two double issues (July/August and December/January). We also have four annual specials: THE FORECAST, THE ESCAPIST and two editions of THE ENTREPRENEURS. Look out for our seasonal weekly newspapers too.

Monocle 24 radio

Our round-the-clock internet radio station delivers global news and shows covering foreign affairs, urbanism, business, culture, food and drink, design and print media. You can listen live or download from *monocle.com/radio* – or wherever you get your podcasts.

Books

Since 2013, MONOCLE has been publishing books like this one, which follows in the footsteps of our best-selling titles *The Monocle Book of Japan* and *The Monocle Book of Gentle Living*. All our books are available on our site, through our distributor Thames & Hudson or at all good book shops.

Monocle Minute

MONOCLE's smartly appointed family of newsletters come from our team of editors and bureaux chiefs around the world. From the daily Monocle Minute to the Monocle Weekend Edition and our weekly On Design special, sign up to get the latest in lifestyle, affairs and design, straight to your inbox every day.

Thank you
Grazie